"This is a much-needed guide to help teens learn how to drop their maladaptive habits of perfectionism, and learn to be kinder and more supportive of themselves. Full of easy-to-understand exercises, this workbook will help teens change the way they relate to themselves so they can start living healthier, more productive lives."

> —**Kristin Neff, PhD**, associate professor of educational psychology at the University of Texas at Austin, pioneering researcher who conducted the first empirical studies on self-compassion over a decade ago, and author of *Self-Compassion*

"The activities contained in this book will help readers to understand perfectionism, and to change the rigid patterns of thinking and behaving that keep it alive. The book is clear, accessible, easy to read, and rooted in evidence-based principles. Teens who struggle with perfectionism will discover practical strategies for letting go and getting on with their lives. Highly recommended!"

> —**Martin M. Antony, PhD, ABPP**, professor of psychology at Ryerson University in Toronto, ON, Canada, and coauthor of *When Perfect Isn't Good Enough*

"*The Perfectionism Workbook for Teens* takes the pain of perfectionism seriously, yet turns the work itself into playful, productive inquiry that expertly guides the young reader (adults, too!) through practical reflections that directly explore the pain, and open some very practical doors to learning, healing, and growth.… From the first page to the last, the workbook is straightforward, intelligent, and creative in its approach; the most effective to be found anywhere. Highly, highly recommended."

> —**Linda Graham, MFT**, author of *Bouncing Back*

"Chock-full of practical and useful exercises to reframe the perfectionistic outlook that keeps you from being your best true self at school, in friendships, and in life. I highly recommend this book to my clients, as well as parents, educators, and therapists."

> —**Christopher Willard, PsyD**, author of *Mindfulness for Teen Anxiety*, and coauthor of *Mindfulness for Teen Depression* , Cambridge Health Alliance/ Harvard Medical School

"This well-written workbook provides a very accessible way to get to know what perfectionism is and how it can affect teens, their families, and friends.… *The Perfectionism Workbook for Teens* provides a format that guides readers to discover if perfectionism is a problem for them.… Parents of teens will find this book to be very helpful in identifying if their daughter or son is having trouble based in trying to be too perfect. Mental health professionals are provided with an evidence-based therapy program that they can include in their practice with confidence. Overall, this is a very useful book that should be widely used."

—**Richard P. Swinson, MD**, professor emeritus in the department of psychiatry and neurosciences at McMaster University, medical director of the Anxiety Treatment and Research Clinic at St. Joseph's Healthcare Hamilton, and coauthor of *When Perfect Isn't Good Enough*

the perfectionism workbook for teens

activities to help you reduce anxiety & get things done

ANN MARIE DOBOSZ, MA, MFT

Instant Help Books
An Imprint of New Harbinger Publications, Inc.

Publisher's Note

This publication is designed to provide accurate and authoritative information in regard to the subject matter covered. It is sold with the understanding that the publisher is not engaged in rendering psychological, financial, legal, or other professional services. If expert assistance or counseling is needed, the services of a competent professional should be sought.

Distributed in Canada by Raincoast Books

Copyright © 2016 by Ann Marie Dobosz
        Instant Help
        An imprint of New Harbinger Publications, Inc.
        5674 Shattuck Avenue
        Oakland, CA 94609
        www.newharbinger.com

Cover design by Amy Shoup

Acquired by Wendy Millstine

Edited by Karen Schader

Activity 19, "Healthy Ways to Motivate Yourself," is adapted with permission from the work of Kristin Neff (http://www.self-compassion.org).

Library of Congress Cataloging-in-Publication Data on file

Printed in the United States of America

22   21   20

10   9   8   7   6   5   4

contents

introduction

You picked up this book for a reason. Maybe you've noticed that you're incredibly hard on yourself, or you never allow yourself to feel happy about any of the amazing things you accomplish. Perhaps you procrastinate or avoid studying, practicing, or social events out of fear you won't perform "perfectly." There are a lot of ways perfectionism can get in the way of you living the life you want!

This book can help. In the activities that follow, you'll learn how to identify healthy and unhealthy aspects of your perfectionism, and you'll develop tools to overcome the negative effects (such as those described in activity 13, which is based on the work of psychologist Rick Hanson). You'll find ways to stay motivated and accomplished without being so self-critical. You'll learn techniques to feel more confident and relaxed in social situations, and you'll develop tools to stop procrastinating and to reduce anxiety about trying new things or making mistakes.

Perfectionism is not a mental health disorder like anxiety or depression; it's a personality trait, like being outgoing, conscientious, or impulsive. Perfectionism is an aspect of your personality—it's not all of you. In this book, you'll learn to see your inner perfectionist as a part of you and find different ways to talk back to this part. You don't have to believe everything that voice says or do whatever it tells you to do. It's amazing what can happen when you find the freedom to respond to that voice in a new way.

Everyone's experience of perfectionism is unique, and so no one person will relate to *all* the activities and tools in this book. Some techniques will work for you and some won't. After using some tools, you may notice a change right away; others you may need to repeat and practice quite a bit before you feel different. You get to discover the path that is right for you, and there will be bumps and obstacles on your journey. There's no "perfect" way to change your perfectionism.

Congratulations on taking the first step toward changing your unhealthy perfectionist habits! Ready to keep going?

1 defining perfectionism

consider this

Do you have high standards for yourself or others? Do you want to get good grades or perform well? Are you ambitious and wanting great things for your life? Wonderful! These are all qualities of "healthy perfectionists" or "healthy strivers."

Perfectionism can also be unhealthy and can lead to anxiety, depression, and real difficulty achieving those ambitious goals you've set. Here are some signs of unhealthy perfectionism:

- You feel horrible about yourself when you fall short of your goals.

- You avoid starting homework, going to parties, or joining teams because you're afraid you won't be perfect.

- You're worried that others will be disappointed or stop caring about you if you make a mistake.

- You feel angry when other people are less than perfect.

Like most people, you probably feel like a healthy striver sometimes and struggle with unhealthy perfectionist feelings at other times. (If you're still not sure whether you're a perfectionist, you can try taking the quiz that's available at http://www.newharbinger .com/34541.) As you read this book and explore your perfectionism, pay attention to which thoughts, feelings, and behaviors are helping you accomplish your goals and be your best self, and which are getting in your way and making you miserable.

look inside

Answer these questions as honestly as you can. Circle the answer that most closely matches your own inner thoughts and beliefs, not the one you think is "right."

Making mistakes is:

A no fun, but bound to happen sometimes.

B not acceptable! It's a sign that I'm not smart enough or good enough.

When I get all As or perform well:

A I feel proud of myself and take a minute to celebrate.

B I feel relieved for a second and then immediately worried about my next goal.

Practices, rehearsals, and classes are:

A fun! I enjoy the process of learning.

B something to get through. I'll be happy when I succeed.

Struggling or feeling sad:

A happens to everyone from time to time.

B isn't okay. I should be happy all the time.

When I imagine failing at something important:

A I know it'll be tough, so I'm glad I have friends and know ways to make myself feel better.

B I worry that I won't be able to handle it and I will fall apart.

When I think about starting a new activity:

A I feel curious and open. Maybe I'll be good at it and maybe I won't, but I'll try my best and see what happens.

B I feel dread and anxiety. If I'm not great at it right away, I'll be devastated.

What makes me *me*?

A I have a lot of unique traits and good qualities, like kindness and a good sense of humor.

B I am the sum total of my grades, awards, and accomplishments.

How many As did you circle? These are some aspects of healthy striving. How many Bs felt more true? These are signs of unhealthy perfectionism, which can affect you in ways like these:

- *Distressing thoughts.* Perfectionism can cause distorted thinking, like a belief that all mistakes will lead to disaster, or a habit of noticing only the negative things in your life. You can get stuck thinking about the past or worrying about the future. You can overidentify with your accomplishments and believe you're only as good as your grades, trophies, or awards. These distorted thoughts can stop you from trying new things, building resilience, and feeling good about yourself.

- *Emotional pain.* Struggling with unhealthy perfectionism often leaves you feeling worried, sad, angry, or hopeless. Sometimes these feelings can get intense or overwhelming. At other times you may try to shut out certain emotions you believe you "shouldn't" feel, and that hurts too. These unhealthy emotional patterns can contribute to anxiety, depression, eating disorders, or other mental health concerns.

- *Destructive actions.* Like a lot of perfectionists, you may wrestle with procrastination, avoidance, overpreparing, and other habits that prevent you from accomplishing your goals. You may also find yourself fighting with friends, having trouble sleeping, restricting your eating, or overexercising as a result of your perfectionist thoughts and feelings.

dig deeper

How does perfectionism help you, and how does it hurt? For each area of life below, write down two or three ways that perfectionist traits (such as having high standards or expectations of yourself or a strong work ethic) benefit you, and two or three ways perfectionism gets in your way.

	How Perfectionism Helps Me	How Perfectionism Hurts Me
School		
Family		
Friends		
Romantic relationships		
Sports, art, or other activities		
Other areas (for example, spiritual life or eating habits)		

Read over all the helpful aspects of perfectionism you listed. Take a moment to let yourself feel good about all these strong, positive qualities. (If feeling proud is tough for you, check out activities 13 and 14.)

Now review the unhelpful qualities you wrote down. These are things you might want to work on changing with the help of this book. Write down five goals you want to work toward, using positive language that describes what you want *more* of ("I want to feel more spontaneous and relaxed") rather than negative language about what you want to *reduce* ("I want to spend less time planning what I wear, do, and say").

1. _____

_____

2. _____

_____

3. _____

_____

4. _____

_____

5. _____

_____

As you work through this book, there may be times when change feels difficult, scary, or painful. Those are good times to reread these goals and remind yourself of what you're working for, what's important to you.

what perfectionism feels like 2

consider this

Your inner experience consists of emotions, physical sensations in your body, and thoughts. There are many emotions you could feel, but they're all related to the core emotions of anger, disgust, fear, joy, sadness, and surprise. Physical sensations can be anything you feel in your body, from muscle tension to a headache to a "gut feeling." Thoughts are more complex ideas your brain cooks up, such as observations, judgments, or beliefs.

If it seems like these three things are really connected and hard to separate, that's because they are. Emotions create physical sensations and lead to thoughts. Thoughts sometimes cause physical sensations or emotions. Physical sensations can lead to emotions or thoughts. It's a circle, each element affecting another. For example, fear (emotion) about an upcoming test could lead to a headache (sensation) and a belief that you aren't smart enough to pass (thought). This circle could just as easily start with the thought, or even the physical sensation.

What does it feel like to struggle with perfectionism? What are the emotions, sensations, and thoughts that make up the inner experience of perfectionism? Everyone's experience is unique, but there are some common threads.

look inside

These emotions are often felt by perfectionists. Circle the ones you have felt in the last six months. Use a single thin line for emotions you've felt once or a few times; use a thicker marker or put multiple lines around emotions you've felt more often.

Worried	Competitive
Afraid	Jealous
Angry	Guilty
Frustrated	Embarrassed
Anxious	Ashamed
Nervous	Tense
Dread	Dissatisfied
Sad	Aggravated
Depressed	Irritated
Hopeless	Stressed
Disappointed	Panicked

dig deeper

Look at the emotions you circled above, especially the ones you circled many times or with the thickest marker. As you remember those feelings, you're probably remembering some physical sensations and thoughts that you experienced at the same time. Pick four of the most common or troubling perfectionist emotions you feel. Use the space below to describe how your perfectionist thoughts, emotions, and sensations are intertwined, as shown in the example provided.

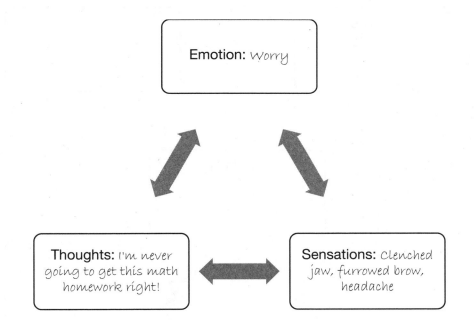

Emotion: Worry

Thoughts: I'm never going to get this math homework right!

Sensations: Clenched jaw, furrowed brow, headache

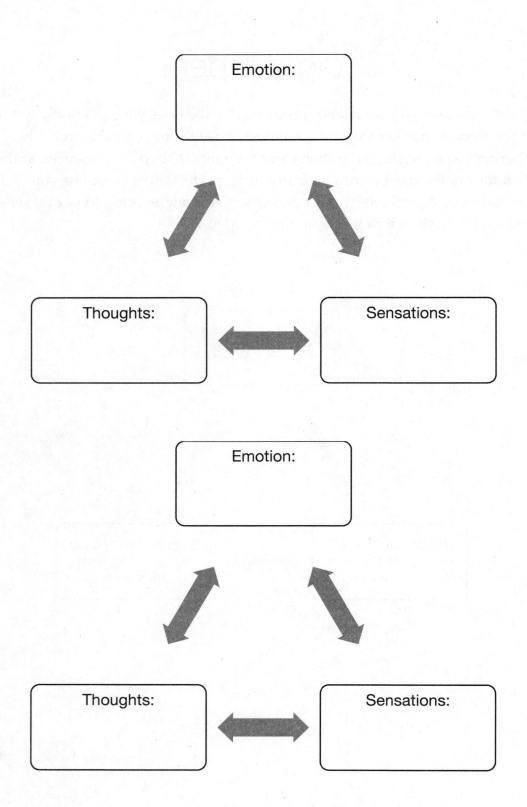

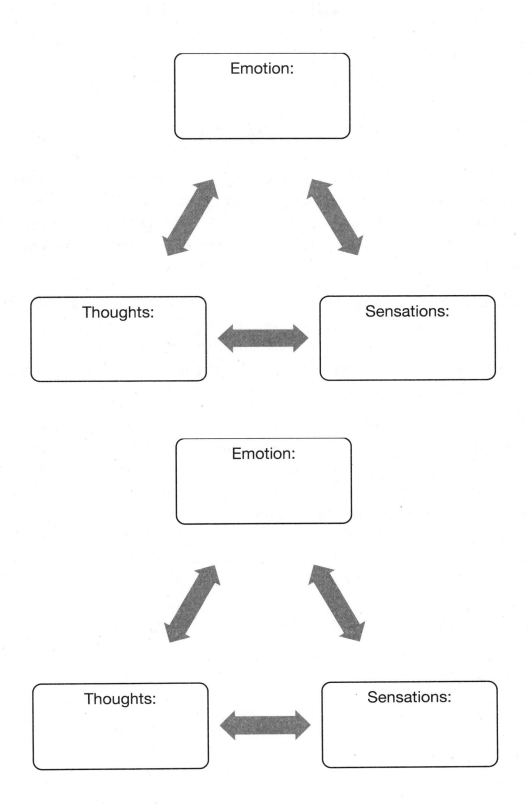

3   what perfectionism looks like

consider this

Annie struggles with perfectionist traits, especially when it comes to writing. She has impossibly high standards for herself, striving to make every writing assignment for school creative and flawless. Even though she is gifted and lots of people love her writing, deep down Annie secretly believes she is no good at all.

Whenever Annie even thinks about writing she feels anxious and afraid. Her fear is so strong that she's been avoiding working on an important English paper by doing all her other homework first, then moving on to checking social media. Some evenings she even falls asleep without meaning to, waking up hours later when there's no time left to work on her paper.

When Annie stops thinking about the paper and checks her phone or does her math homework instead, she experiences momentary relief—it feels great to stop worrying for a while! But in a short time that relief fades and the fear is back, stronger than ever. She ends up writing her paper the night before it's due and makes several careless mistakes because she was rushing. She gets an average grade and sees this as further evidence that she's actually not a very good writer. She feels even more anxious about the next paper.

look inside

Emotions, thoughts, and sensations are inner experiences, and behaviors are the external actions we take to deal with what's going on inside. Perfectionism can create a lot of strong feelings, like Annie's fear and anxiety, or other emotions like sadness, anger, or guilt. To try to reduce those unpleasant feelings, Annie engages in procrastination, a common (and unhealthy) coping technique that results in short-term relief but increases problems in the long run. Perfectionists often use other unhealthy coping techniques like these:

- *Planning or organizing excessively*. You run out of time to actually get things done, or feel panicked when things don't go according to your plan.

- *Overworking*. You lose out on sleep or fun because you're trying to make a project or performance perfect, or you actually make something worse through constant revising.

- *Controlling*. You have really strict rules for yourself around eating, exercise, appearance, or other areas of life, in hopes of feeling "in control" of everything.

- *Avoidance*. You skip social activities, games, tests, or other obligations out of fear you won't perform perfectly.

Can you think of a time when you engaged in each of these perfectionist behaviors? How did they help you in the short run, and how did they hurt in the long run?

I procrastinated when: _____

_____

How it helped in the short run: _____

_____

How it hurt in the long run: _____

_____

I planned or organized excessively when: _____

_____

How it helped in the short run: _____

_____

How it hurt in the long run: _____

_____

I overworked when: _____

_____

How it helped in the short run: _____

_____

How it hurt in the long run: _____

_____

I controlled when: _____

_____

How it helped in the short run: _____

_____

How it hurt in the long run: _____

_____

I avoided when: _____

_____

How it helped in the short run: _____

_____

How it hurt in the long run: _____

_____

dig deeper

Reread your descriptions above, and try to remember what emotions you were feeling before you engaged in each of these behaviors. Describe the underlying emotions here:

Procrastination:_____

_____

Planning or organizing excessively:_____

_____

Overworking:_____

_____

Controlling:_____

_____

Avoiding:_____

_____

What are some things that help when you're feeling these difficult emotions? For each emotion, write down two activities that have helped you feel better in the past.

Emotion	Healthy Action
Example: _Anxious_	_Go for a run_
	Ask a friend for a hug
Example: _____	_____
	_____
Example: _____	_____
	_____
Example: _____	_____
	_____
Example: _____	_____
	_____
Example: _____	_____
	_____

Next time you feel the urge to engage in perfectionist actions, try one of the ideas you wrote down above. Notice whether addressing the underlying emotion helps you. For example, do you procrastinate less or do the thing you avoided?

4 there's more to school than grades

consider this

For perfectionists, school can be a series of landmines. You're constantly being evaluated, graded, ranked, and compared to your peers. This can create or strengthen beliefs that your value depends on those numbers and titles. If you have labels like "gifted" or "captain" next to your name, you might feel enormous pressure to perform at a certain level at all times, like you never get to rest, never get to let your guard down. Exhausting!

After a while, the pleasure you used to feel playing a sport or instrument, solving equations, or writing poetry fades, and all you pay attention to is the scorecard. When grades and ranks and scores are everywhere, it's easy to focus on those things and forget about other stuff that also matters.

look inside

Think about some of the classes, sports, or other activities where you strive for perfection. What drew you to these things initially? If grades and scores were eliminated, what would you still enjoy about each activity?

Activity	Things I Love
Example: _Play drums_	_Get lost in the flow of music, fun to move around a lot_
Example: _____	_____
Example: _____	_____
Example: _____	_____
Example: _____	_____
Example: _____	_____

How do you feel as you read through this list? What's it like to reconnect to your feelings of joy, fun, and other positive feelings? Write down what thoughts and feelings you notice as you read the list:

_____

_____

_____

Pick one activity from the list, and promise yourself to focus on what you love about it this week. At the end of the week, write here about how it went. Did you have trouble remembering your intention? Were you able to feel more pleasure or fun during your activity?

_____

_____

_____

dig deeper

Grades, scores, and evaluations can make you feel good about yourself. It feels great to get approval and praise from others! However, when you rely on *only* those external sources for self-esteem, you build a fragile and vulnerable structure that can get knocked down by a strong wind. A bad grade or lost game feels devastating and may make you question your worth as a person. You may become more susceptible to depression, anxiety, and other mental health issues. To create a solid frame of self-esteem that can withstand a storm, you need to draw on internal sources of value and pride.

What do you like about yourself that can't be ranked, graded, or scored? What makes up the foundation of your self-esteem? Is it your compassion or kindness? Your sense of humor? Your love of learning? List your favorite qualities about yourself in the foundation lines below.

If you would like, add in grades, awards, or titles as decorative elements—for example, doors or windows. You can be proud of those things too, but they are not the foundation of your self-esteem!

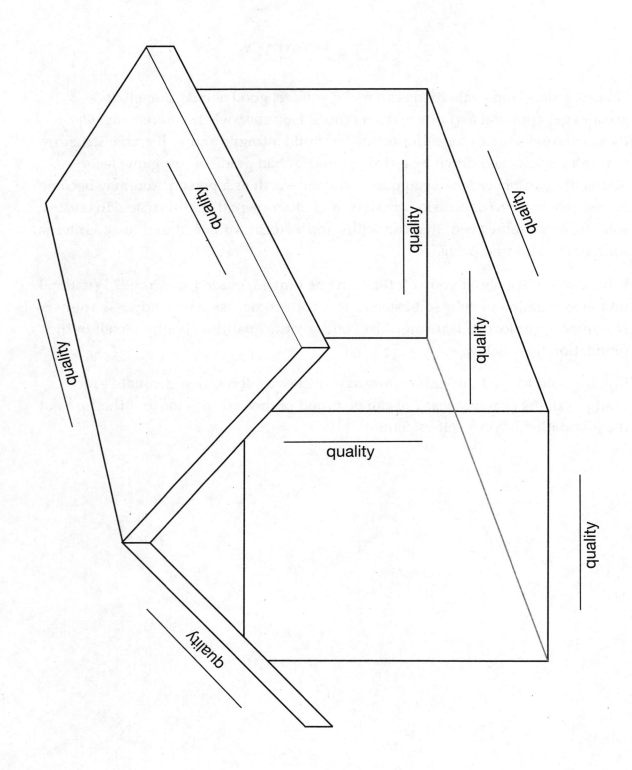

messages from family: 5
carrying the perfectionist torch

consider this

The things your parents and other family members say and do have a big impact on your personality. You shape your beliefs about yourself in part based on what your family expects from you. Praise, comments, and criticisms from them can become voices in your head, telling you what's right or wrong, acceptable or shameful.

Have you heard or seen things in your home that gave the impression that your family is expecting perfection from you? Maybe your parents seem focused on that one B-plus and don't say much about all the As on your report card. Perhaps it feels nearly impossible to live up to a successful older sibling. You might have observed your parents criticizing themselves or someone else for not meeting impossibly high standards. If it seems like your parents expect perfection or something close to it, you can find yourself adopting those standards for yourself, carrying the perfectionist torch they handed to you.

look inside

What are the perfectionist messages you feel have been handed to you by your family? Write down things that parents, siblings, or other family members have said or done that resulted in your feeling pressured to be perfect. These might be direct comments, hints, or actions. They may even be messages they didn't intend to send.

Example: <u>When I got a C on a midterm, Dad said he was disappointed and</u>

<u>knew I could do better.</u>

Example: <u>My sister was voted student council president and has a million</u>

<u>friends.</u>

_____

_____

_____

What is the perfectionist value you believe you were handed in that moment?

Example: <u>The only way to be successful is to be perfect.</u>

Example: <u>The measure of how good you are is your level of popularity.</u>

_____

_____

_____

_____

dig deeper

The values you inherited from your family may be ones they intended to impart. Or they may have been trying to communicate something positive but the message got garbled on its way to you. However those messages got there, you now have a choice to make. Are the perfectionist values you were handed ones you want to keep? Part of moving through your teen years and becoming an adult is examining the beliefs and ideas you learned from your family. You get to decide what you want to keep as yours and what feels like something to let go of or modify to make your own.

Take some time to think about the values you listed above. Are the messages you learned from your family all ones you want to keep as your own? Or is there another way of thinking that fits you better? Rewrite the values you listed above in a new way, a way that works better for *you*. Or write new ones!

Example: <u>For me, success means working hard and doing my best, and it</u>

<u>doesn't matter so much what grade I get.</u>

Example: <u>Quality of friendships matters more than quantity!</u>

_____

_____

_____

_____

6 gender and perfectionism

consider this

Perfectionism doesn't discriminate based on gender, sexuality, race, or religion. Anyone can struggle with perfectionist traits! But the struggle often looks different depending on your gender. Society, family, culture, and religion can send very different messages about how guys should look and act versus how teen girls or young women should be. Perfectionists can take those messages and "shoulds" to heart and really stress themselves out trying to fit "perfectly" into their gender role. Young people who identify as genderqueer or in another nonbinary way can also get anxious about meeting some personal or social expectations of "perfection."

Jenna has an image in her mind of the perfect teen girl. The image is a composite of several celebrities: tall, thin, with perfect hair and more expensive clothes than Jenna can afford. In an attempt to transform herself into this ideal, Jenna denies herself breakfast and lunch, works out for hours every day after school, and weighs herself three times a day in hopes that she will hit her "target weight" soon. Jenna feels dissatisfied with herself pretty much all the time.

Will's vision of the perfect guy is someone who is great at every sport he tries, super strong and fast, and a good leader. Will is captain of his basketball team at school; he's pretty decent at soccer and baseball, but he wants to be better. He spends extra time at the gym after practices, ignoring the homework he's supposed to do or his plans with his friends. He pushes through injuries, even though his coach tells him to rest. He gets so anxious before games he often throws up, worried that he's going to make a mistake.

Lisa's friends all know her as the best shoulder to cry on, the most understanding ear in the whole school. Anyone who has a problem goes to Lisa. She loves this role and wants to be perfect at it. When a friend texts with a problem, Lisa stops whatever she's doing to answer, even when it means missing out on sleep she needs or abandoning commitments she made. When her sister asks for help with homework, Lisa drops hers and often doesn't get back to it before the night is over. When she can't fix someone else's problems, Lisa thinks about it constantly, wondering what else she could have done.

look inside

Jenna, Will, and Lisa are all struggling with perfectionism, and their images of the ideal young man or woman shape how their perfectionism expresses itself. Jenna believes she should be thin and traditionally beautiful. Will believes the ideal guy is a strong leader and in perfect physical shape. Lisa believes the perfect young woman always puts others before herself.

What is your idea of the perfect young woman? How is this similar to or different from the examples above?

_____

_____

What is your idea of the perfect young man? How is this similar to or different from the example above?

_____

_____

Do you have an idea about what "perfection" looks like for someone who is androgynous, genderqueer, intersex, or identifies in another way? Describe it here.

_____

_____

Ideal images like these can lead to unrealistic expectations of yourself and others. Jenna expected herself to look like this ideal image, even when it was physically impossible to change her height and body type. Will expected to excel at everything; Lisa expected she could fix every problem she encountered, even the unfixable ones.

Read your description of "perfection" for your gender identity. Which "ideal" qualities do you expect of yourself? How realistic do you think these expectations are, on a scale of 1 (not at all realistic) to 10 (totally realistic)?

"Ideal" Quality	Rating

dig deeper

Unrealistic ideals and expectations can lead to unhealthy behaviors. For Jenna, it's destructive dieting; for Will, it's overexercising; for Lisa, it's abandoning her own needs to take care of others. What are the negative consequences of these behaviors?

Dieting excessively: _____

Exercising excessively: _____

Putting others first all the time: _____

Write down any possibly unhealthy behaviors you've noticed in yourself as you pursue your ideal gender role. Next to each, write down the possible negative consequences of that behavior.

Unhealthy Behaviors	Negative Consequences
_____	_____
_____	_____
_____	_____

thinking critically about cultural messages 7

consider this

You undoubtedly see dozens of images a day, in advertisements, articles, and videos. You read as many messages, online and off, and hear even more in songs. Many of those pictures and words are trying to convince you there is something wrong with you, so you'll feel the need to buy some product that will improve you. They're designed to awaken any thoughts about being imperfect and needing to change. In short, they're designed to awaken your inner perfectionist!

look inside

What can you do to change how these messages affect you? You can start by becoming more aware of the messages you're taking in and the impact they have on you. When you see an ad or a video, read something online, or hear a song, pause and check out how you're feeling inside. Do you feel happy, calm, or relaxed? Do you feel anxious, down on yourself, or sad? What thoughts are going through your head? Are you longing for something to buy or some way to change yourself? Do you notice tension in any part of your body?

To explore this, gather some old magazines that you can cut apart. As you flip through the pages, cut or tear out any images or words that make you feel like something is wrong with you, or that you need to improve. Paste these images onto a plain piece of paper, making a collage of cultural messages. You can also print images out from websites or write in phrases you hear in song lyrics, on TV shows, or elsewhere.

As you look at all the images and read the words, pay attention to what happens inside you. Is your inner perfectionist awake and trying to get your attention?

What thoughts are you having as you look at your collage?

_____

_____

What emotions? _____

_____

What body sensations? _____

_____

Once you're aware of the impact the culture has on you, you can start making choices to reject the perfectionist messages and invite in healthier, more realistic words and images. It's not easy, and the negative messages will still get through sometimes, but making an effort to let in the positive can create some balance.

Look through magazines or websites again. This time, search for images and words that make you feel happy with yourself the way you are now. These may be hard to find! If you can't find many, try writing your own. Create a second collage on a new piece of paper.

Look at the images and words on this new, more positive collage.

What thoughts are you having as you look at your collage?

_____

_____

What emotions? _____

_____

What body sensations? _____

_____

dig deeper

Was it easier to find negative images and phrases or positive ones? Why do you think that is?

_____

_____

_____

_____

Now that you have spent some time with the positive, healthier messages, look at your first collage again. Can you use the strength of those positive thoughts and feelings to prevent the perfectionist messages from getting to you? What's different about your experience this time? Write down what, if anything, has changed in your thoughts, feelings, or sensations.

_____

_____

_____

appearances deceive 8

consider this

Pressure to be perfect can come from lots of places, like school, family, and movies, among others. Pressure can also come from friends—even if they are not intending it! The way you and your friends talk to each other about your homework or activities, your struggles or achievements, can create another whole layer of expectations that feel impossible to meet.

In your school or your group of friends, it may seem that you not only have to do everything perfectly but also have to appear as if you did it all effortlessly. Friends may downplay how much they studied to make it look like they aced a test without trying, or pretend they put no thought into their appearance when in fact they agonized over outfits, hair, and makeup. Pictures and posts to social media give the appearance of a life filled with beauty, fun, and no problems. The more people put up the appearance of being "perfect" without breaking a sweat, the more that expectation gets ingrained into you and all your friends.

What's behind this desire to present a perfect face to the world? Sometimes people are afraid of appearing vulnerable by admitting they are struggling. Many just want to fit in. There's always a reason underneath, something your inner perfectionist is trying to accomplish by putting on this deceptive appearance.

look inside

Think about a time when someone appeared to be effortlessly happy or successful. Maybe you got this message through things you saw in person or on social media, or something the person said. Describe what you saw or heard that led you to believe that person was effortlessly perfect in this situation.

_____

_____

_____

How do you feel as you remember this situation? Describe your thoughts, emotions, and sensations. Notice especially if you felt the pull to create a similar effortless appearance yourself.

_____

_____

_____

How realistic is your perception of effortless perfection? Is it possible that there are problems or struggles you aren't seeing? Describe some alternate possibilities.

_____

_____

_____

Think of a time you exaggerated how easy something was or tried to appear effortlessly perfect. You may have done this with words, pictures, or actions. Describe it here.

_____

_____

_____

The desire to appear perfect without trying usually comes from some kind of anxiety about fitting in, being accepted, or looking strong and capable to others. What was the motivation behind _your_ perfect face? What were you hoping to get others to believe about you?

_____

_____

_____

dig deeper

When you fudge the truth and create a false image of perfection, you actually make yourself *more* anxious, not less. It's exhausting to put up a false front all the time! And the more you pretend to be something you're not, the more you secretly believe that who you are is not good enough. You might feel anxious or ashamed, or doubt your ability to withstand the normal ups and downs of your life.

How do you break out of the pattern of putting on a "perfect face"? Tell your truth! Being honest about what's hard, about feeling sad or stressed, often feels like a relief, like a weight being lifted. And often when one person starts telling the truth, others feel permission to take off their masks and be real too.

Go back to the situation you described above. If you could have a do-over and be honest and vulnerable about your truth, what would you say? What different pictures would you show on social media? What other actions would you take? Rewrite your story here, or draw a more realistic image of yourself on a separate piece of paper.

_____

_____

_____

_____

_____

_____

_____

How you tell your story is important, but it's also important to think about who is listening. When you're being honest and real, you're being vulnerable, which can open you up to getting hurt. You want to choose safe and trustworthy people to see the real you. Who are the people in your life you trust to see your vulnerable self?

_____

_____

_____

Can you choose one person on that list to be real with this week, to talk honestly with about difficult feelings or struggles you're having that you would normally mask? Describe what happens here. What are the thoughts and emotions you have when you get real with this person?

_____

_____

_____

9   the biology of perfectionism

consider this

Perfectionist thoughts, self-criticism, and anger at others don't exist just in your head. These thoughts, emotions, and beliefs have a strong impact on your body—your nervous system, muscles, heart, and lungs react to what's going on in your head. Likewise, the way you're feeling physically has a strong impact on your thoughts and feelings. When your body is pumping stress chemicals, it's pretty hard to feel happy and relaxed.

So what happens in your body when you're suffering from perfectionist stress? You have a worry about, say, performing well at a concert, and your brain and body respond as if there is a life-or-death situation, like you're about to be eaten by a tiger. Your sympathetic nervous system—your fight-or-flight system—gets activated, sending cortisol and other stress hormones flooding through your body. Your heart rate and breathing quicken, your muscles tense. Your brain becomes vigilant for any new threats and starts seeing danger everywhere. You actually become biologically more likely to think negatively! And the more negative thoughts you have, the more your fight-or-flight system gets activated—a vicious cycle of negative thoughts, emotions, and sensations.

look inside

Breaking the cycle of perfectionist stress starts with awareness. For each of the common perfectionist emotions below, write down what you notice happening in your body; use the blank line to add any other emotion. Pay attention to *where* in your body you feel the emotion, and describe *what* you feel. Does that feeling have a shape, size, color, or other visual component in your imagination? What do you notice about your breath or heartbeat, and about your overall energy level?

Emotion	Where I Feel It	What It Feels Like	What I Visualize	My Breathing or Heartbeat	My Overall Energy Level
Example: Fear	In my eyes and my arms	My eyes feel wide open, my arms feel tense. Twitchy	I imagine a bright white-yellow color.	I'm breathing pretty fast and my heart feels like it is pounding.	I feel jumpy and nervous.
Anxiety or worry					
Anger					
Disappointment					
Sadness					
Other _____					

dig deeper

What is it like to be more aware of what you're feeling in your body when you're having perfectionist thoughts? Sometimes just noticing and naming the sensations you're feeling can be enough to lower the intensity and break the cycle of stress. Other times you may need to take more action to experience a change in your physical experience.

When your sympathetic nervous system is fired up, you can try this simple breathing exercise to engage the parasympathetic nervous system instead—the part of your nervous system responsible for resting and relaxing.

Calming Breath

Start by creating a quiet space for yourself, where you won't be interrupted for three minutes. Put your phone on silent, turn off any music or other noise. Close your eyes if you're comfortable doing so. Inhale through your nose to a count of four. Now exhale slowly and smoothly through your nose to a count of eight. When your lungs are empty, pause for a beat before you inhale again. Repeat this cycle five more times.

After you complete six rounds of calming breath, check in with yourself. What are you aware of now?

_____

_____

Are you still feeling the emotion you felt before the breaths? Do you feel it less, more, or the same?

_____

Describe any changes in the emotion below.

Where you feel it in your body: _____

_____

What it feels like: _____

_____

How you visualize it: _____

_____

Your breathing or your heartbeat:_____

_____

Your overall energy level: _____

_____

worrying doesn't cause 10 success

consider this

David had a big project to do in the first semester of his advanced English class. The teacher mentioned it at the beginning of the semester but said not to worry about it yet; the details would come in a couple of months. David did worry about it though. He thought about it often and would sometimes comment to friends that he didn't see how he was going to make time for this big project on top of all his other homework. His friends didn't seem stressed and told him to relax, that he'd get it done like he always did.

After the teacher gave the details of the assignment, David kicked his worrying into high gear, thinking about the assignment when he fell asleep at night, in the shower, and on the bus to and from school. When he texted his friends about it at odd hours, they told him again to stop worrying so much. David was annoyed with his friends because he "knew" that if he didn't worry and stay on himself like an overbearing parent, he wouldn't get the work done. In the end, David got an A on his assignment. Several of his more relaxed friends also got As. David gave most of the credit to his constant thinking and worrying about the project.

You may think, like David did, that his worrying actually contributed to his success. But this is an example of a common thinking error: *superstitious belief.* Just because thing A happens before thing B does not mean that thing A *caused* thing B. It's similar to acing a test and crediting your good grade to the T-shirt you put on that morning. David worried and stressed before working hard and getting a good grade, but that worry did not *cause* him to do good work or get the good grade, any more than your T-shirt helped you pass the test.

Not only does thing A not cause thing B, but sometimes thing A can actually make thing B even harder. Repeated negative thoughts and high stress levels often do more harm than good. When you're stressed, you flood your brain and body with stress chemicals that make you less able to think and perform well, and make succeeding in most activities less likely. You would likely be more productive and do better work if you felt calm, believed in yourself, and gave yourself some regular breaks between work sessions.

look inside

Check out the common perfectionist superstitious beliefs below. Circle the ones that sound familiar to you.

If A	Then B
If I worry all week	then I'll do well on the test
If I let myself take a break	then I'll become very lazy
If I am really hard on myself	then I'll be motivated to get a lot done
If I get average grades on some subjects that are not priorities	then I'll start slipping in every subject

What are some other things you believe you "have to" do in order to succeed?

If A	Then B

Pick three outcomes from the above list—items from column B that are important for you to achieve or avoid. For each, list at least two things (other than your superstitious belief) that would help you achieve that goal.

Outcomes	Alternate Action
Example: _do well on a test_	_study effectively_
	get some sleep
Example: _be productive_ _during homework time_	_make a study schedule_ _study with a friend so I am accountable_
Example: _____	_____
	_____
Example: _____	_____
	_____
Example: _____	_____
	_____
Example: _____	_____
	_____

dig deeper

Sometimes the best way to test whether a belief is true is to run a little experiment. David came up with the following experiment to test his belief about worrying:

> *For the second semester of his English class, David decided to try studying and working on his final project without constant worrying. This was hard because the worried thoughts came whether David wanted them to or not! But whenever he noticed himself worrying, David would say "Not now" to the worried thought and tell himself he could think about the project during his scheduled English project time (Tuesdays and Thursdays for one hour in the evenings). He accepted his friends' invitations to go out on weekends. At the end of the semester, David got an A on his final project.*

Would you be willing to test out one of your superstitious beliefs to see how true or not true it is? Choose one of the outcomes from your list of three above. Write up the rules for an experiment to test your belief. Eliminate your superstitious behavior (like David's worrying) and replace it with your alternate plan (David made a study schedule and let himself take breaks with his friends). Try to make a plan you can complete within a few days, or a few weeks at the most. Write out your plan:

_____

_____

_____

What was the outcome of your experiment?

_____

_____

_____

11 it's okay to make mistakes

consider this

Mistakes are a natural part of the learning process. Everything that works had a period—sometimes a long period—when it didn't work. Thomas Edison had a thousand failed attempts at making the light bulb before he figured it out. Oprah Winfrey was fired from an early job as a television reporter because she was too emotional for the news. J. K. Rowling received dozens of rejections for her first Harry Potter book before finally getting a yes. Michael Jordan was cut from his high school basketball team.

What all these people had in common is that they didn't let mistakes crush their spirits or prevent them from trying the next thing. Mistakes give you the opportunity to learn something new, to do better next time, to come up with creative solutions to get out of jams. They also help you build confidence, as you rack up experience in overcoming obstacles and setbacks. If you don't allow yourself to take risks and make errors, you stay stuck in your comfort zone, and fail to grow and learn. In addition, letting go of your fear of making mistakes allows you to approach tasks with ease and enjoy yourself, instead of being superfocused on performing perfectly.

look inside

The fear of failing often touches very big, deep fears. You see a small mistake and your mind gets carried away. You imagine the consequences getting worse and worse: a snowball rolling downhill getting bigger and faster until it's an avalanche. Choose two areas of life where you're afraid of making a mistake, and follow that fear down to its roots.

Example—Area of concern: <u>Getting into college</u>

If I: <u>do not get accepted to my top choice college</u>

then: <u>I will have to go somewhere less ideal</u>

then what?   <u>I will be unhappy and feel bad about myself</u>

then what?   <u>I'll get depressed and fail out of college</u>

then what?   <u>I won't succeed in work or even be able to support myself</u>

then what?   <u>I'll die young, alone, and miserable.</u>
(worst possible consequence)

Area of concern: _____

If I: _____

(mistake or failure)

then: _____

(consequence)

then what? _____

then what? _____

then what? _____

then what? _____

(worst possible consequence)

Area of concern: _____

If I: _____

(mistake or failure)

then: _____

(consequence)

then what? _____

then what? _____

then what? _____

then what? _____

(worst possible consequence)

Looking through these lists of consequences, how realistic do they seem? Try writing the stories out in a more realistic way:

Example—Area of concern: Getting into college

If I: _do not get accepted to my top choice college_

then: _I will go to another good school_

then what? _I will feel sad for a while, but then find things I like about my school_

then what? _I'll do well in my classes and make friends_

then what? _I'll find a career I like_

then what? _I'll enjoy my life, and it won't matter that I went to college B_

instead of A.

activity 11 ✳ it's okay to make mistakes

Area of concern: _____

If I: _____
(mistake or failure)

then: _____
(realistic consequence)

then what? _____

then what? _____

then what? _____

then what? _____

Area of concern: _____

If I: _____
(mistake or failure)

then: _____
(realistic consequence)

then what? _____

then what? _____

then what? _____

then what? _____

dig deeper

The story of the cracked pot is based on an old myth attributed to several different wisdom traditions. It goes like this:

A girl has two large pots for carrying water from the river. It's her job to get water for her family every morning. She places the pots in the exact same way every day, side by side in an open wagon, and walks them up the path to her house. One of the pots is "perfect" and always arrives as full as it was when pulled out of the stream. The other pot has cracks in it. Water leaks out slowly the whole walk back, and the pot arrives at the house half full.

The perfect pot is very proud of himself for carrying water so flawlessly. He's certain he is more admired and liked than the other pot. The cracked pot feels ashamed of herself and is certain her imperfections will lead her to be tossed out with the garbage any day.

After a year of leaking and worrying, worrying and leaking, the cracked pot couldn't take it anymore. Down at the river, she spoke to the girl: "I am sorry I am so flawed. I am ashamed of myself."

"Why are you ashamed?" the girl asked.

"I have all these cracks, and water leaks out of me the whole trip up the path. I arrive half full and worry you won't have enough water for the day."

The girl smiled and said, "As we walk back to the house, look at the right side of the path and the left side and tell me what you see."

The cracked pot watched as the wagon bumped and rolled up the path. On the right side, where the cracked pot always was, beautiful wildflowers lined the edge of the path; on the left side there was just dirt and occasional tufts of weeds.

At the end of the walk, the cracked pot still felt guilty for wasting so much water and apologized again. She said, "If you want to replace me with a better pot, I'll understand."

The girl responded, "No way! I love you the way you are! I noticed your cracks last fall, and that's why I planted all those wildflower seeds on your side of the path. I knew the water you leaked would help them grow. I've had fresh flowers for the house every day this spring. And I have traded flowers with neighbors for juice and milk, so I don't need as much water at the house. So you see, none of your water has been wasted, and my life is so much better with you in it!"

How do you feel as you read this story? What thoughts, emotions, and sensations do you notice?

_____

_____

_____

What are your cracks, mistakes, and flaws? How do your unique features benefit you or the people around you, or make the world a more interesting and beautiful place?

_____

_____

_____

perfectionism and self-esteem

12

consider this

If you're a perfectionist, chances are you work really hard and you accomplish a lot. But like many perfectionists, you probably also have a difficult time actually feeling good about all that hard work or your positive qualities. Maybe you have a secret belief that you aren't *really* smart or talented. Or maybe you think that expressing pride or confidence is the same as being arrogant or conceited.

Healthy self-esteem means having a realistic understanding of your strengths (as well as areas you want to improve), taking pride in your efforts, and feeling confident about your abilities. It means valuing your work ethic, your motivation, your creativity, your intelligence, your kindness, and your other positive traits. You may get recognized for these qualities—for example, with grades, awards, or titles—but healthy pride is more about appreciating your underlying character, rather than relying on external markers of accomplishments. Healthy pride makes people want to be closer to you. Confidence is attractive!

Being proud of yourself is *not* the same thing as arrogance. Arrogance is an unrealistic view of yourself—exaggerating good qualities and denying any areas for improvement—or focusing on titles, awards, and grades rather than character. Even though it might seem like arrogance comes from self-esteem that is too high, it actually comes from *low* self-worth. When you feel insecure and bad about yourself, you sometimes overcompensate in hopes that creating an image of yourself as awesome will help you feel awesome on the inside. (Hint: this doesn't work!) Arrogance pushes people away.

We all have moments of feeling high self-esteem and moments of feeling insecure. Check out the lists below for tips on how to express pride in healthy ways.

Healthy Expressions of Pride	Unhealthy Expressions of Pride
Viewing your strengths realistically	Exaggerating achievements or skills, fixating on being the best or being perfect
Having confidence in your abilities	Downplaying your skills in hopes that others will contradict you (fishing for compliments), or asking for reassurance all the time
Feeling comfortable expressing pride when you do well	Hiding pride in complaints or "humble brags" ("Ugh, I have so many extra practices because I was chosen for this all-star game!")
Being aware of faults or weaknesses, and open to change and growth	Feeling angry or ashamed when areas for improvement are brought to your attention, or blaming others for mistakes
Expressing gratitude for your skills, qualities, and accomplishments	Feeling entitled, or expressing anger when you have a less-than-perfect performance

look inside

For each scenario, circle the description of healthy pride or self-esteem. On the blank lines, write down what qualities make it a positive, healthy statement or action.

Kiara just found out she is a finalist for a prestigious science scholarship. The next step in the application is to write a fairly lengthy paper describing an experiment and the outcomes. Kiara posts on social media:

A "Don't expect to see me at anything fun this weekend. Stuck inside writing this annoying paper for a full-ride scholarship."

B "I can't believe I made it to the final round of this scholarship application! It's been a lot of hard work. Wish me luck writing this super tough paper this weekend."

_____

_____

Maya worked hard all summer to get in shape for soccer. It's the first practice of the season, and she does well on some complicated drills that really tripped her up last year. She turns to her teammate and says:

A "I made it! Last year I literally fell on my face in this exercise. I am so glad I did all those sprints and footwork practice this summer. It really helped!"

B "Ugh, I can't believe how clumsy I am! I still suck so bad! What do you think?"

_____

_____

Connor is trying out for the lead in the play. He did great in past performances and has done a lot of research and rehearsal for this part that he wants. As he's getting ready to audition, he thinks to himself:

A *I'm a shoo-in for this part. No one else trying out is remotely as good as I am.*

B *I've got acting experience and I put a lot of time and effort into preparing for this audition. I feel really good about my chances.*

_____

_____

Jordan is frustrated that she can't get the fingering right on a difficult guitar chord and keeps messing up her solo. The rest of the band seems disappointed that the song isn't coming together, and that they may have to cut it from their set list for now. Jordan says:

A "Sorry guys, this is a tough chord and I think I need more practice before I can count on getting it right."

B "Who wrote this stupid solo? The chord changes are impossible! It's not my fault it sounds so bad."

_____

_____

dig deeper

Think of a time you felt pleased with how hard you worked or with a difficult goal you achieved. Describe the situation here.

_____

_____

_____

Was it easy to feel proud of yourself, or did you feel worried about appearing arrogant? What were your worries about what others would think or say?

_____

_____

_____

Following the examples above, think of a healthy way of expressing pride in this situation. Write it out here.

_____

_____

_____

Now try it out with a trusted friend or family member. Check in with that person after. Did your fears about being seen as arrogant come true?

13 never good enough?

consider this

Life is a series of "what's next." You get a new phone, and you immediately start thinking about when the next version will come out. You ace the midterm and then start worrying about the final. You have a fun date with someone you like, and as soon as it's over you're stressing about what you'll say the next time you see each other. Any of this sound familiar? Don't worry, you're not alone...

Susie gets great feedback on her public-speaking presentation. She thinks, "It's a good thing I stayed up all night rehearsing, instead of relaxing like my mom suggested." She doesn't let herself enjoy the feedback because she believes she has to be hard on herself all the time to stay motivated.

Scott worked hard all fall semester and gets all As as a result. When he sees the grades, he feels a wave of pride, but it's immediately interrupted by thoughts of the next semester's classes, which will be even harder. He starts worrying about how he can find a little more time to study in his already overloaded schedule.

Zara steps back to look at her finished painting. A big smile appears on her face as she delights in the color, composition, and feel. She stops herself from smiling, telling herself it's conceited to be so proud of her work. She starts picking apart the painting, finding little flaws and thinking about how she can do better next time.

look inside

Setting new goals and continually improving is great—but when you don't make time to really take in your achievements and feel proud of yourself, you get trapped in a vicious cycle of never feeling happy, never feeling good enough.

Research shows that really sitting with a good feeling, like pride or accomplishment, and letting yourself fully feel the emotion can start to break the "never good enough" cycle. It doesn't take long—only about twenty to thirty seconds—to start to make an impact. Building this habit of letting yourself feel good can slowly, with time and repetition, make your brain less quick to jump to negative thoughts and feelings, and help positive emotions flow more freely.

Take a moment now and remember a recent achievement. Let yourself feel proud, excited, relieved—whatever positive feelings come up. Set a timer and savor the feeling for thirty seconds; even exaggerate them if you can! Describe the experience below. Notice how your body felt, what emotions came up, and what thoughts you had as you sat with your positive emotions.

_____

_____

_____

dig deeper

You can also acknowledge and celebrate accomplishments in bigger ways, for longer than thirty seconds, and with others present. Think of some other recent achievements of which you feel proud. Did you do well in a game or match, create an interesting piece of art or music, pass a hard class? Now think about what you did to acknowledge or celebrate that achievement. Did you tell a friend or family member? Did you reward yourself with an hour of video games or a movie out with friends? Did you take a few moments to just sit and feel happy? If you didn't do anything, write down what you would like to do to honor that achievement.

Achievement: _____

Celebration: _____

Achievement: _____

Celebration: _____

Achievement: _____

Celebration: _____

You might notice a part of you, a voice inside, telling you that you don't deserve rest or celebration, that you should achieve more first. That perfectionist part of you probably has a long history of saying these things, and it will take some time to change that habit. Try to acknowledge the voice, and tell it "Not now" or "No thanks." There are more specific tools for talking back to the voice coming up later in this book.

learning to accept 14
a compliment

consider this

Lots of people are uncomfortable receiving a compliment or praise. We blush, feel embarrassed, or don't know how to respond. Perfectionists tend to have a *really* hard time and engage in all sorts of mental gymnastics to turn praise into something negative. Feeling bad about yourself is a more familiar feeling for perfectionists, and we sometimes prefer what's familiar even when it feels terrible.

> *Kaitlyn played a strong game and scored the winning goal. As soon as people started to congratulate her, she felt uncomfortable. Her cheeks grew red, and she found it hard to look people in the eye. Even though they were all saying positive things, what she heard was unspoken criticism of the few things she did "wrong" or less than perfectly. She dismissed their praise with comments about how she could have done better and hurried off to the locker room to be alone.*

> *After a party, a friend smiles and pats Josh on the shoulder, telling him that he made a good impression on the girl he likes. As he hears his friend complimenting him, Josh's anxiety starts to rise. "Oh no, now my friends are going to expect me to be the life of every party. And this girl is going to expect me to be funny and charming all the time. I can't live up to that!"*

> *Miranda shows her mom her report card. Miranda had brought up some midsemester Bs and now her final grades are all As and A-minuses. Mom smiles and says, "You did great, honey!" Instead of seeing the smile and hearing the kind words, Miranda hears an unspoken message that Mom wouldn't love her as much if she brought home average grades.*

They all went through some mental maneuvering to turn praise into criticism, anxiety, or a threat. Have you ever felt uncomfortable when you received a compliment or praise, and gone through mental gymnastics to get past the discomfort?

look inside

Write down a compliment, praise, or a positive message you heard from someone in your life—perhaps a family member, friend, teacher, or boss. On the next line, write down the unspoken criticism, threat, or hidden message you heard.

What was said: _You're so smart; I know you'll get all As!_

What I heard: _If you get a B, I'll be disappointed._

What was said: _____

What I heard: _____

What was said: _____

What I heard: _____

What was said: _____

What I heard: _____

What was said: _____

What I heard: _____

dig deeper

Learning how to take a compliment is an important part of feeling happy, and it also makes others feel good too. Far from making you conceited, graciously accepting a compliment with a "Thanks, I worked hard on this. Your painting is awesome too!" shows that you have self-confidence. It also makes compliment-givers feel much better than when you dismiss their praise.

Look at the list of compliments you just wrote down. Replay those moments when you got the praise, and see if you can press "pause" before the mental gymnastics start. Slowly reread the compliment and try to take it at face value, to really hear what the person was saying. Let yourself feel good for at least twenty seconds instead of pushing those positive feelings away.

Next, record each compliment on your phone and play it back to yourself. Look in the mirror as you hear it and practice saying thanks without giggling nervously, dismissing the comment, or looking away. As a final step, ask a friend to say each line, and practice looking that friend in the eye and saying thanks.

15 the power of apology

consider this

Do you aim to be a perfect friend, son or daughter, boyfriend or girlfriend? Does the thought of hurting someone else's feelings—even accidentally—make you want to hide under the covers and never speak to that person again? Of course, none of us want to hurt people we care about, and it's wonderful to strive for kindness toward everyone. But it's basically impossible to have a close relationship with others and never cause them pain, even accidentally. Any two people who care about each other will hurt each other's feelings at some point in their relationship. The important question is: what do you do *after*?

Psychology researchers have found that relationships that have solid repairs—sincere apologies and meaningful change to address problems—are healthier and stronger than relationships where it seems like nothing goes wrong in the first place. Making mistakes and then repairing them actually strengthens relationships and builds trust!

So how do you make a repair that strengthens your relationship? You start with a healthy apology, which means three things: regret, responsibility, and remedy. Regret means a sincere "Sorry" or "I apologize." Responsibility means naming what you did wrong, and how it impacted the other person—"I forget your birthday, and I let you down." Remedy means offering a way to right the wrong—fixing what you broke, promising to do better in the future, or asking how you can make it up to your friend.

Not all apologies are healthy, however, and if you're missing the elements above, you may end up saying "I'm sorry" in a way that keeps the wound open instead of healing it. These are some common aspects of unhealthy apologies:

- *"But"s and "if"s.* Apologies lose their power when you follow them with "but" and an angry defense of your actions. Similarly, saying "I'm sorry if you were hurt" also weakens your message.

- *Taking too much responsibility.* Overapologizing ("OMG, I'm the worst friend ever! I'm sooo sorry! I suck so bad.") can sound insincere or can make the other person feel like now she has to make *you* feel better.

- *Avoiding.* It's natural to feel upset, embarrassed, guilty, or any number of emotions after you hurt someone or make a mistake. It's tempting to avoid the subject or dodge the person so you don't have to deal with it. This can keep the wound open and painful, instead of resolving and healing the hurt.

look inside

Read the following scenarios and responses. Which option is the best repair to strengthen the relationship?

Your friend Dylan is wearing a sweater that is a little tacky. When you see him at lunch, you crack a joke. His face falls, and he tells you his grandma who just passed away made it for him.

A *"I'm so sorry! I'm always making bad jokes and making everyone feel horrible. I'm an awful friend."*

B *Change the subject and try to make jokes about something else to get him to laugh and like you again.*

C *"Oh man, I'm sorry. That was a really insensitive thing to say. I know your grandma meant a lot to you. I won't make jokes like that again."*

You're in a bad mood after school. You walk in the door, and your mom asks you how your day was. You snap at her, then go into your room and slam your door shut.

A *"Hey Mom, I'm sorry about snapping at you before. I was in a bad mood and I took it out on you. My day was kind of crappy. Can I talk to you about it now?"*

B *Hide in your room the rest of the evening, feeling embarrassed about the way you reacted.*

C *"I'm sorry if you felt mad about what I said. I was just trying to answer your question!"*

You skip your friend's birthday party because you're just not up for hanging out with a big group of people that night. You hear from someone else that your friend is upset you didn't come.

A *"I'm sorry if you were hurt, but you had so many people coming it seemed like you didn't care if I was there or not."*

B *"I'm really sorry—I didn't mean to make you feel like I don't care about you, because I really do. Can I take you out for coffee and ice cream tomorrow?"*

C *"I'm a terrible person; all I do is hurt people. I understand if you never want to talk to me again."*

After you identify the healthy apology in each scenario, label the regret, responsibility, and remedy in the statement.

dig deeper

Is there a recent situation where you wanted to apologize but avoided it or said something that seemed to make the situation worse? Take a moment now to briefly describe the situation.

_____

_____

_____

Write out a healthy apology. Remember: regret, responsibility, remedy.

_____

_____

_____

What happens when you imagine delivering the apology in real life? Notice if you feel tense, anxious, excited, or worried, or have some other feelings. Whatever you're feeling is okay!

_____

_____

_____

Can you try delivering this apology to the person who needs to hear it?

focusing on the journey, 16
not the destination

consider this

At any given moment, there are a million things happening around you. Pause right now and look around…notice the color of the walls or the sky. Maybe you hear the sound of music playing or the hum of a fan blowing. There is so much going on that you can't possibly be fully aware of all of it at once! Every moment you make decisions about what to bring forward (perhaps the music?) and what to let fade into the background (the hum of the fan).

At this moment, there are many experiences going on *inside you* as well. Usually sensations like your heart beating and your lungs breathing fall into the background, and in the foreground are your thoughts and some of your more intense emotions. You can't pay full attention to everything all the time, so you choose certain feelings and thoughts and sensations to focus on, and you ignore others. Most of the time you aren't even aware of making the choice. And more often than not, you focus on negative thoughts and emotions over positive ones.

All people have this *negativity bias*, this predisposition to look out for potential or current danger, stress, or other negative experiences. There's a good reason for this—as humans evolved, it was more important to remember dangers (where the tiger lives) than the good stuff (where the juicy mangos are). If you forget where the mango is, you'll live another day and find something else for lunch, but if you forget where the tiger is, you *become* lunch.

Perfectionists are even more likely to focus on what's wrong and filter out what's pleasant or good. Often any sign of joy or accomplishment immediately triggers fear, worry that letting yourself feel happy or relaxed will lead to letting down your guard, missing signs of danger, or becoming "lazy." So you focus on the negative and ignore the positive, and think, *I'll let myself feel happy later—after I pass the class*. Or graduate or win the game or get the job or…

The problem with putting off happiness until tomorrow is that tomorrow never comes. There's always another goal or milestone in the future, another reason to put off feeling good *now*. Learning how to let yourself enjoy this moment, in all its imperfections, is a crucial step toward lowering your stress or depression, and increasing your sense of well-being.

look inside

Find a safe place where you won't be interrupted for five minutes. Stop and look around you; scan your external environment. Write down five pleasant or positive things you observe, as well as five neutral or unpleasant things:

Pleasant or positive:

1. _____

2. _____

3. _____

4. _____

5. _____

Neutral or unpleasant:

1. _____

2. _____

3. _____

4. _____

5. _____

Now scan your internal experience. Notice sensations, thoughts, and emotions. Write down five things you notice that are pleasant or positive; for example, a sense of feeling rested, relaxed muscles, happiness, or a thought about some fun plans later tonight. Write down five neutral or unpleasant inner experiences too; for example, feeling sad, worrying about an upcoming test, or a stomachache.

Pleasant or positive:

1. _____

2. _____

3. _____

4. _____

5. _____

Neutral or unpleasant:

1. _____

2. _____

3. _____

4. _____

5. _____

What did you notice while engaging in this exercise? Was it easier to notice negative things in the environment than positive? Was it easier to notice negative internal experiences than pleasant ones?

_____

_____

_____

Did you notice any thoughts come up to try to talk you out of feeling good? For example, a voice saying that this small pleasure doesn't matter, or that it's not safe to be happy because you'll get lazy? Write your thoughts below.

_____

_____

Pause and notice your five pleasant experiences once again. Set a timer for two minutes and spend about twenty seconds focusing on each pleasant thought, emotion or sensation. Really soak in how each one feels. When the timer goes off, write down how you feel.

_____

_____

_____

dig deeper

To build your capacity to feel happiness, you need to practice noticing the good in the present moment. Pick a simple activity that you do several times a day—something like turning a key in a lock or washing your hands. Each time you engage in that activity, pause and scan your internal experience, and notice at least three positive sensations, thoughts, or emotions. Alternately, you can set an alarm on your watch or phone to go off three to four times a day, and scan your experience whenever you hear your alarm.

Keep all your observations together in a positivity journal. This is a place to record all the things that make you feel happy, proud, and grateful—from the sensation of sun on your face to the thrill of finishing school for the summer. You can write in a blank notebook, on your phone, or on scrap paper. Recording pleasant experiences helps you be more aware of the good stuff in life. You can also read your positivity journal during tough moments, when you feel overwhelmed by negative emotions.

you don't have to be good at everything 17

consider this

Brianna has always found that music comes to her easily. She seems to have natural skills and can learn almost any instrument quickly after picking it up for the first time. She finds it hard to really enjoy her musical gifts though, and instead focuses on activities that don't come naturally to her, like sports. She spends so much time beating herself up over not making the soccer team that she is too bummed to enjoy playing the solo in the fall orchestra concert.

Jacob expects perfection in all areas of school and life. He doesn't accept anything less than an A in any subject, even those he doesn't like and those that don't have much connection to what he wants to study long-term. Jacob spends hours and hours trying to get his grades up in math classes and doesn't have time to work on his personal creative writing projects. He suspects he could be a great writer, if he could just accept a B-plus in math class and let himself spend those hours writing instead.

Ana started high school this year and wants more than anything to be at the top of every class, club, and sports team. She studies and practices all the time. She turns down almost every invitation to hang out with friends or go to movies and even rejects an offer from the girl she likes to go to the winter formal dance. By spring semester, Ana is exhausted and burned out. Her group of friends, tired of always hearing no for an answer, have stopped even asking her to do stuff. Ana feels anxious all the time, and her life feels out of balance.

look inside

Take a moment to think about all the things that are important to you. These could be individual classes or areas of study, sports or specific games or tournaments, a creative pursuit, a relationship, or a hobby. Write down these priorities below.

_____

_____

_____

_____

You have a finite amount of time, energy, and attention. If you have three hours a night to spend on homework and you take two and a half hours to finish your chemistry take-home quiz, then you have only a half hour left for everything else. That might be a wise way to divide your time if this is an important quiz, if chemistry is a crucial subject for you, or if your other homework isn't due for a couple of days. However, if the chemistry quiz isn't important, if there are more pressing assignments, or if you need to devote time to practicing the cello for a college audition, that might not be the best use of your time.

In the pie chart below, draw a wedge for each important element in your life. Make wedges of different sizes to show how much time, energy, and focus you would ideally like to spend on each activity. Make sure your pie chart includes:

- sleep

- relaxation and self-care

- family

- friends and fun

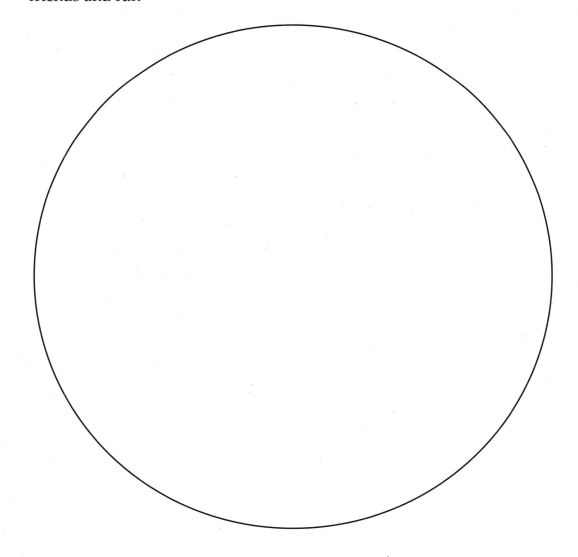

dig deeper

As you can see from your pie chart, there are some important things in life that may not get your full attention. This doesn't mean you should give up completely on things you can't do "perfectly"! It means that there could be a few classes or activities where you may have to accept good work, rather than strive for excellence.

Accepting work or performances that are good but not up to your extremely high standards will likely bring up an internal reaction: maybe a feeling of fear, an inner voice protesting, or a sensation of tightness in your stomach. How do you imagine you might feel accepting good rather than "perfect" in one of the areas on your pie chart?

_____

_____

Think of three things you can do to help soothe those distressed thoughts, emotions, or sensations; for example, going for a run, talking to a friend, taking a bath, or reminding yourself that you don't have to be great at everything to be a good person. Write them here:

1. _____

2. _____

3. _____

consider this

Your brain is a real thinking, computing, creating machine that can do amazing things. That doesn't mean that every thought you have is true. The brain can come up with all sorts of distorted versions of reality, and sometimes even make things up out of thin air! These distorted thoughts, or *thinking errors,* can lead to unpleasant emotions like anxiety and fear, or destructive behaviors like avoidance and picking fights.

Here are some common thinking errors that impact perfectionists:

- *Magnifying and minimizing.* You turn small mistakes or minor obstacles into catastrophes, things to be feared and avoided at all costs, and reasons to beat yourself up when they do occur. You downplay or ignore anything good that happens, denying yourself any pride or relaxation.

- *Mind reading.* You read into what other people say (or don't say), hear hidden messages and criticisms, or assume the worst. Or you try to predict the future based on limited information, assuming disasters or triumphs that aren't realistic.

- *Black-and-white thinking.* You oversimplify, seeing situations in black and white, and ignoring the shades of gray. This thinking error can also include overgeneralizing; for example, deciding that all teachers are mean because one or two are.

- *Labeling.* You turn a behavior (forgetting a birthday, losing a game) into a judgment about you as a person (*I'm a bad friend; I suck at sports*). Or you apply labels to others based on their behaviors (*He's a jerk; she's selfish*).

- *Double standards.* You hold yourself to one set of expectations (perfection) and others to a more realistic standard. Or perhaps you let yourself off the hook, but expect that those around you will never make a mistake or let you down.

look inside

Can you remember times when you experienced some of these thinking errors? You may not have been aware at the time that you were thinking in an unhealthy or unrealistic way—often your brain makes these errors without you even knowing! Read the examples below and write about times when you've had a similar experience.

Minimizing good or magnifying bad

Example: _Aced my chemistry midterm, shoved the paper to the bottom of my_

backpack. Told myself it doesn't matter, it's just a midterm.

_____

_____

_____

Mind reading

Example: _José didn't text me back last night. He's sick of me. I'm too needy._

_____

_____

_____

_____

Black-and-white thinking

Example: <u>I didn't nail the cheerleading tryout routine perfectly on the first try.</u>
<u>It's clear I'm not good at this, so why bother going out for the team.</u>

_____

_____

_____

Labeling

Example: <u>My mom forgot to pick me up from practice after school. She's a</u>
<u>completely unreliable person.</u>

_____

_____

_____

Double standards

Example: <u>My friend got a B on a test, and I told her that was great; she should be</u>
<u>proud. I got a B on a different test and I got really mad at myself, told myself</u>
<u>I'm stupid.</u>

_____

_____

_____

dig deeper

The first step in countering any of these errors is being able to notice them when they are happening, or soon after. Once you catch yourself in the act of thinking in a distorted way, you can choose to respond to those thoughts in a new, healthier way.

Here are some ways you can challenge thinking errors when you catch them:

- *Explore evidence* for and against your thought. Are you really going to fail the class or not graduate because of one bad grade?

- *Get feedback* and perceptions from *trusted* friends and family members. Do they see the situation the same way you do?

- Draw a line and place your black-and-white ideas on either end. Fill in some options in *between the two extremes*:

Example:

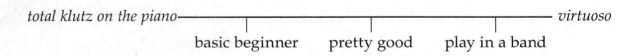

total klutz on the piano————————————————————————— *virtuoso*
basic beginner   pretty good   play in a band

- Write down *what you would tell a friend*. How does it differ from what you tell yourself?

Read through the thinking errors you wrote down earlier. Use the previous methods to write out a new response to each distorted thought.

Distorted thought: _____

Response: _____

_____

Distorted thought: _____

Response: _____

_____

Distorted thought: _____

Response: _____

_____

Distorted thought: _____

Response: _____

_____

Distorted thought: _____

Response: _____

_____

19 healthy ways to
motivate yourself

consider this

Many perfectionists believe that the only way to motivate themselves to work hard enough to stay on top is to use harsh, stress-inducing methods—think of it as "critical coaching." You buy into the myth that if you're gentle with yourself, you'll get lazy and complacent. Or maybe you believe that being kind to yourself is selfish or indulgent. However, being kind and encouraging, praising successes and accepting mistakes—or *compassionate coaching*—actually makes you more motivated and a better friend.

Here's the science: When you're self-critical, put a lot of pressure on yourself, or worry intensely, you often trigger the biological symptoms of fear. Fear can bring on increased heart rate, muscle tension, and elevated cortisol and other stress hormones. When you're afraid or anxious, you have less blood pumping to the parts of your brain that think clearly and form new memories—not a good thing when you're trying to study for a test!

In comparison, when you're relaxed and compassionate, the parasympathetic nervous system (the calming branch of your nervous system) turns on, which research shows leads to higher creativity and better ability to understand complex ideas. More blood flows to the prefrontal cortex, the part of your brain that does most of your thinking. A hormone called oxytocin flows, making you better able to express your caring feelings and feel connected to friends, family, and romantic partners.

Far from making you "lazy," being kind and compassionate toward yourself actually makes you more capable. You're biologically a smarter student, more caring friend, and harder worker.

look inside

How do you motivate yourself? Is it different from how you might encourage a friend or a loved one? Read the following scenarios and imagine what you would typically say to yourself and what you might say in a pep talk to someone else. Write down your statements to yourself on the left side of the paper, and your statements to your friend on the right. You can use the blank line at the end to add your own scenario.

Scenario: Studying for an important final exam, which will have a huge impact on your grade

Talking to yourself: Talking to your friend:

_____   _____

Scenario: Training for baseball or softball tryouts

Talking to yourself: Talking to your friend:

_____   _____

Scenario: Getting up the courage to ask someone on a date

Talking to yourself: Talking to your friend:

_____   _____

Scenario: _____

Talking to yourself: Talking to your friend:

_____   _____

dig deeper

Cover the left side of the paper and read only the statements to your friend. After you have read them all, close your eyes and sit quietly for a moment. Scan your experience…how do your neck and shoulders feel? What sensations do you feel in your chest and belly? Do your arms and legs feel active and ready to move, or still and resting? What emotions are you feeling right now? What thoughts are you having? Write down what you noticed.

_____

_____

_____

_____

Now cover the right side of the paper and read all the statements you'd typically make to yourself. Take a moment to scan your experience again. Write down what you noticed.

_____

_____

_____

_____

What differences did you feel in your brain and body when you read the "compassionate coaching" versus the "critical coaching" sentences?

_____

_____

_____

_____

What do you think might change if you said the compassionate statements to yourself rather than the critical ones?

_____

_____

_____

_____

20 what's your story?

consider this

Makayla believes she is socially awkward and hard to like. This is a story she's told herself for a long time, and every day it seems like something happens to confirm that it's true. Here are some things that happened to Makayla today:

- *In the halls between classes, she tried to talk to a guy she likes, but he walked away just as she approached him.*

- *At lunch a new friend invited her to a party this weekend.*

- *A guy she likes only as a friend asked her out.*

- *Her whole English class laughed at a witty joke she made when she was answering the teacher's question.*

When Makayla was getting ready for bed that evening, she reviewed her day. Makayla remembered approaching the guy she liked and him turning away; she felt hurt and ashamed. Ugh, I'm so awkward and weird, no one wants to be my friend, let alone date me. *She briefly remembered the other guy asking her out but dismissed it as unimportant, since she doesn't like him that way. She forgot about the other positive events of the day.*

Zach's story about himself is that he is really good at math and science, but terrible at English or anything that involves creativity. Here are some things that happened to him today:

- *Zach's friend said she hasn't been able to stop thinking about a comment Zach made about the book assigned for English class, and asked if it's okay if she uses that idea in her paper.*

- *In biology class, Zach got great feedback on his paper. The teacher said Zach explained some complex concepts in an easy-to-understand and unique way.*

- *He got his test back in English class and cringed at the C-plus on the top of the first page.*

Zach was having a hard time falling asleep because he kept thinking about that C-plus, alternately calling himself stupid and telling himself that English is lame and there's no point in even taking that stupid class. He thought, That comment I made to my friend was the one original thought I'll ever have about books. *I'm hopeless. It didn't even occur to him that his success on his bio paper was in large part due to his creative thinking and ability to write well.*

look inside

Each of us creates an *internal working model* of ourselves, a story about what we're good at and what we're bad at, our natural strengths and weaknesses. While there is usually some truth to these stories—math does come more easily to Zach than writing or reading—we often exaggerate these stories and see ourselves in black and white rather than shades of gray.

As your internal model gets solidified, you notice only events and feelings that fit into your story about yourself, and disregard all the things that don't fit the model. You ignore the positive events altogether, or you make up reasons why those experiences don't really matter—like Makayla did when that guy asked her out.

What do you believe about your social abilities? What story do you tell yourself about how skilled or clumsy you are socially?

_____

_____

_____

What do you believe about your intellectual capacity? What ideas do you have about your natural strengths and weaknesses?

_____

_____

_____

What story do you have about your physical strengths and weaknesses?

_____

_____

_____

What do you believe about your creativity?

_____

_____

_____

Do you have a story about your spiritual self? Your religious or ethical self? Do you believe you're naturally "good" or "bad?"

_____

_____

_____

dig deeper

Can you think of something that has happened lately that goes against your internal working model of yourself? A good grade in a subject you think you aren't the best at, a new person reaching out to you despite your belief that you're bad at meeting new people? Write down some recent events that counter your stories about yourself.

Social: _____

_____

_____

Intellectual: _____

_____

_____

Physical: _____

_____

_____

Creative: _____

_____

_____

Spiritual, religious, ethical: _____

_____

_____

Did you notice a voice inside arguing with you as you wrote down the evidence against your stories, telling you these facts are unimportant, or an exception to the rule? Did you have trouble thinking of any examples at all?

Pick one area of life where you have a fairly rigid story about yourself; for example, social, physical, or creative. For the next three days, keep your antennae tuned to any evidence that goes against your internal working model. If you'd like, you can ask a friend to help you with this, to point out any times you have success in the realm you chose. Write down everything you notice here.

_____

_____

_____

_____

_____

21 thoughts aren't always true

consider this

Thinking is what the brain does, just like breathing is what the lungs do. Sometimes your thoughts are meaningful, sometimes they're silly and inconsequential. Some thoughts are based on accurate observations and provide real wisdom. Others are based on overwhelming emotion and can be distorted and confusing.

How can you tell which is which? If an image of a Chihuahua in a dress pops into your head—something you saw online yesterday—it's obvious it's one of the silly thoughts that doesn't mean anything. It's easy to laugh and let the thought go. Other times it's not so easy to tell whether you should take a thought seriously. For example, you think your friend is mad at you, and it's hard to figure out whether that's a true thought based on evidence (she *did* have a weird look on her face) or a distorted thought based on anxiety (you're often worried about people getting mad at you, even when there's no reason for them to be upset).

The more emotionally charged a thought is, the easier it is to get pulled into believing it wholeheartedly. Imagine your thoughts are waves: The simple thoughts are small waves, and it's easy to let them splash up against you or roll right past you while you stand still, feet on the ground. The real emotional thoughts are bigger waves that can knock you down or sweep you out to sea. You no longer feel grounded and in control; you're at the mercy of these thoughts taking you wherever they are going. But with practice, you can learn to keep your footing during big and small waves alike.

look inside

Thoughts, just like waves, come and go; they don't stick around forever. Watching the waves can be a helpful way of understanding that *you* and *your thoughts* are separate. Your thoughts are something you have and you can observe; you are not your thoughts. You can begin building your ability to observe your thoughts by trying this basic mindfulness meditation practice. Start out during a calm, low-stress time of day.

Watching the Waves

Find a space where you can sit quietly for about four minutes without being disturbed or distracted. Turn off your phone and other devices. Sit comfortably, with your feet on the floor and your back upright. Set a timer for three minutes. Close your eyes and focus on your breath. Picture your breath moving in and out of you—coming in through your nose, down into your chest and belly, and then moving back up and out of you. Visualize this for ten cycles of inhale and exhale.

Now let go of your focus on your breath, and bring your attention to your mind. What thoughts do you notice? Picture your thoughts as something moving in and out of your mind, just as you did with your breath. Imagine each thought is a wave slapping against you as you stand still, feet on the ground.

When you realize you've become absorbed in a thought—if you've been knocked down or carried away on one of the waves—simply notice that it's happening and put your feet back on the ground, return to observing your thoughts. A really important part of this—and a part that is really hard for perfectionists!—is to do this *nonjudgmentally*. Perfectionist patterns may cause you to judge yourself for doing this exercise "wrong" or beat yourself up for being "bad" at mindfulness. If you notice those judgments, try to observe them and let them pass by you as well. These are just more waves moving past you and through you.

Continue to observe your thoughts until the timer goes off. Before you get up and move on, take a moment to notice how you feel. Is there anything different about your body, your emotions, or your thoughts after you spent these three minutes observing?

Keep practicing this basic technique at least once a day for a week. Choose calm moments, when you're not experiencing many stressful thoughts or feelings. You can try extending the time to four or five minutes, or try this meditation practice during more challenging times of the day, when big waves of perfectionist thoughts are crashing into you.

dig deeper

Once you've had some practice sitting and observing your thoughts, you're ready to try the next step, naming your thoughts. Naming is another way to build some distance between you and your thoughts.

Naming the Waves

Start the same way you did before—find a comfortable place where you won't be interrupted, and turn off your phone and other devices. Set a timer for three minutes, or longer if you'd like. Focus on your breath; picture it moving in and out of you. Then turn your attention to the waves of your thoughts, some lapping gently around you, some crashing hard into you.

This time, as you notice each thought arise, give it a *simple* name before letting it go. If you notice the thought *I can't remember if I locked the door when I left*, name it "worrying." If you start thinking about what you're doing next, name that "planning" and let it go. When perfectionist thoughts arise, name them and let them go. Don't get too involved in choosing which label to use—if the right name isn't obvious within a second or two of noticing the thought, just call it "thinking," let it go, and return to observing.

When the timer goes off, pause for a moment before getting up and going back to your life. What was it like naming your thoughts? Did you notice a theme to the type of thoughts that arose?

Repeat this practice once or twice a day over the next week. Do you notice differences in the kind of thoughts that arise, or how easy or challenging it is to let them go?

22 identifying what triggers your perfectionism

consider this

Observing your thoughts come and go, like waves splashing into you and rolling past you, can be a powerful tool in battling perfectionism. You can use this technique when you're sitting still, practicing mindful meditation as described in the last activity. You can also use this tool throughout the day, when you're hanging out with friends, playing a sport, participating in a class discussion, or doing pretty much anything. This is often called an informal mindfulness practice, because you keep doing what you're doing, while your observing "program" runs in the background, noticing thoughts arising and falling. An informal mindfulness practice can help you get a little distance from your perfectionist thoughts in those moments you need it most.

Observing your thoughts during daily life can also help you learn what situations are triggers for your perfectionist thoughts and feelings. By paying attention to your thoughts throughout the day—noticing, naming, and letting go—you can start to see patterns. Maybe you notice that being alone brings up more perfectionist beliefs, or maybe they come up more strongly when you're around other people. You might see that competitive sports or difficult school subjects bring with them lots of big waves that tend to knock you down. Knowing your triggers can help you be more prepared, so you can go into those challenging activities ready to counter those unhealthy perfectionist thoughts before they get the better of you.

look inside

Pick two activities that will be happening regularly over the next week. These can be as simple as brushing your teeth or more complex and challenging, like attending a class or going to a party. Don't choose the most difficult tasks, or ones that require your full attention. You need to be able to pause as needed to notice, name, and let go of your perfectionist thoughts as they arise.

Write down the two activities you will use to practice informal mindfulness:

_____

_____

Before each activity, pause and remind yourself of your intention to observe your thoughts. As the activity starts, keep your inner antennae tuned to your thoughts, especially perfectionist thoughts. Give 95 percent of your attention to your class or party or whatever you're doing, and keep 5 percent of your attention on observing what's happening in your mind.

When you notice a perfectionist thought arise, take a moment to name it, and then imagine it rolling past you like a wave. At first you might need to pause, close your eyes for a moment and concentrate, then return to whatever you're doing. With practice, you will be able to notice, name, and let go of your thoughts while staying fully engaged in your activity of the moment.

As the thoughts arise and fall, notice how big or small the waves are, how easy or difficult it is to let them go. As soon as possible after the event is over, record the thoughts you remember. Were you able to observe them? Did you start to argue with them? Did you believe them and start to feel sad or stressed?

Examples:

Event: <u>Basketball game</u>

Thought: <u>After my friend missed a shot, I thought about all the times he goofed</u>

<u>off in practice.</u>

What happened: <u>Got really mad, thought about all the angry things I wanted to say</u>

<u>to him, took me a few minutes to notice and label it as perfectionist thought.</u>

Event: <u>History test</u>

Thought: <u>If I don't get an A, I'm a stupid idiot.</u>

What happened: <u>Noticed the thought while it was happening, and let it go.</u>

Event: _____

Thought: _____

What happened: _____

Event: _____

Thought: _____

What happened: _____

Event: _____

Thought: _____

What happened: _____

Event: _____

Thought: _____

What happened: _____

Event: _____

Thought: _____

What happened: _____

dig deeper

As you look over these different events, do you notice any patterns? Are there certain events that are more challenging than others? Were certain kinds of thoughts easier to let go, and others more likely to knock you over and pull you along for a while? You may want to pick a few more activities during which to practice informal mindfulness and see if any more patterns emerge.

Look through all the thoughts you wrote down for all your informal mindfulness sessions. Write down the most painful or stressful thoughts here.

_____

_____

_____

What do these difficult thoughts have in common? Did these thoughts happen during the same kind of activity?

_____

Do the more challenging thoughts arise on a certain day or time of day? If so, when?

_____

Who were you with when you had your most difficult thoughts? Or were you alone?

_____

If you noticed any other pattern, what was it?

_____

_____

Now look through your original list of thoughts again. Write down the perfectionist thoughts that were the easiest to let go, the ones you were able to watch roll on by with ease. Write those down here.

_____

_____

_____

What do these easier thoughts have in common? Did these thoughts happen during the same activity, at a certain time of day, or with certain people? Write down any patterns you notice.

_____

_____

_____

What have you learned about which situations are more likely and less likely to trigger perfectionist thoughts?

_____

_____

_____

_____

23 getting to know your inner perfectionist

consider this

Observing yourself helps create some distance between you and your thoughts, between you and your perfectionism. Sure, your critical, demanding, competitive thoughts are *part* of you, but they are not *all* of you. There is a bigger you—an observing self—that can watch those perfectionist thoughts come and go.

By mindfully observing your thoughts, you can start to see your perfectionist part as more and more separate from that observing self. Your inner perfectionist can sort of become a person you can talk to. You can learn to set limits when your perfectionist self is being pushy, and offer comfort when that part of you is freaked out and scared. It takes a lot of repetition to create this distance between your observing self and your inner perfectionist, so try not to be hard on yourself or get impatient if it doesn't happen right away, if you still catch yourself identifying with the perfectionist messages and doing what the voice says.

look inside

Create a perfectionism journal to take everywhere with you for three days. You can write in a blank notebook, make notes on your phone, or simply use a sheet of paper. Write down any perfectionist thoughts you notice. Start with this moment, right now. Pause and notice what thoughts are rolling through your mind. Is your inner perfectionist demanding that you do this activity perfectly? Is that voice worried that you're falling behind on your homework by reading this book? Write down what you are observing right now—this is the first entry in your perfectionism journal.

Over the next three days, use your informal mindfulness skills to notice any perfectionist thoughts as they arise. To help you remember, you may want to list specific events or activities coming up that may trigger your inner perfectionist and make a reminder to pay attention to your thoughts at that time. Or, you can set an alarm on your phone to go off three or four times a day, and take a few minutes to write down all the perfectionist thoughts you remember having in the last few hours.

dig deeper

Read through the statements you wrote down, the things your inner perfectionist said to you over the past few days. As you read, can you imagine what your inner perfectionist's voice sounds like? Is it gruff and demanding? Loud and obnoxious, or whiny and anxious? Write a description of the voice in the space below. Read the thoughts again and imagine the way your inner perfectionist looks. Write down any other details you imagine: maybe the voice always seems to be coming from over your left shoulder, or perhaps you imagine this part has a certain smell. Let your imagination run free as you picture your perfectionism as a separate, distinct being.

Finally, use the space inside the box to draw an avatar for your perfectionist. Maybe you draw the way the perfectionist looks in your mind's eye, or maybe you create some other image that represents your inner perfectionist. Imagine you're creating the profile pic for your perfectionist's social media account. Finally, give your inner perfectionist a name.

Voice: _____

Face: _____

Body: _____

Clothes: _____

Size: _____

Age: _____

Anything else? _____

_____

Name: _____

24 how is your inner perfectionist trying to help?

consider this

As you start to gain distance from your perfectionist thoughts and see that those thoughts are coming from a distinct part of yourself, you probably feel curious about who this inner perfectionist is and why this part exists. Why is some part of you acting so mean, scared, and demanding?

Good question! As hard as it may be to believe sometimes, your inner perfectionist is trying to help you. Your inner perfectionist is trying to motivate you to work hard, or to act a certain way so other people will like you. This part is trying to earn love, avoid rejection, or feel in control.

However, the way this part goes about achieving these goals is not always the most efficient or the most kind. Beating you up, denying you any relaxation or joy, making you feel constantly angry and disappointed with everyone around you or with yourself—these methods may be somewhat successful, but they cause a lot of collateral damage. It's like using a hammer to press the "on" button on your computer or cell phone. You may be successful in turning the device on, but you'll smash the keyboard or screen in the process. When your inner perfectionist uses harsh methods to motivate you, it can damage your mood, your self-esteem, your relationships, your health, and more.

look inside

What positive things is your inner perfectionist trying to do for you? In the spaces below, write down some of the thoughts, emotions, and behaviors you've identified as part of your perfectionist self. Next to each one, write down the benefits you get from each. See the examples below to help you get started.

Perfectionist Thought, Emotion, or Behavior	Benefit
Spend an hour writing and rewriting a text to a guy I like, so it sounds exactly right	Feel certain I didn't say anything embarrassing or stupid
Thinking that if I get less than an A on this assignment, I'm a failure	Read the chapter twice, double check my work, get an A

dig deeper

The benefits you get from your inner perfectionist's actions come with a price. For each action you listed above, write down the collateral damage that comes along with it.

Perfectionist Thought, Emotion, or Behavior	Damage
Spend an hour writing and rewriting a text to a guy I like, so it sounds exactly right	Late to pick up my sister and didn't have enough time to finish my homework
Thinking that if I get less than an A on this assignment, I'm a failure	Feel anxious all week and have trouble sleeping. Feel bad about myself until I get the test back and see my grade.

As you read over all the ways your inner perfectionist is trying to protect you and keep you safe, what thoughts and emotions do you notice?

_____

_____

_____

Pick one benefit from above—like wanting to get a good grade or feel confident in a social situation—and think of three other ways you could achieve that goal without the collateral damage.

1. _____

2. _____

3. _____

25 how do you respond to your inner perfectionist?

consider this

As you've discovered, your perfectionist voice is a *part* of you, not *all* of you. That part of you has thoughts and feelings and is trying to accomplish something for you (although usually in a pretty mean way!).

You have other parts inside you too. One of those is an observing part that can see and hear what the perfectionist part says—and can respond to it. There are a lot of ways people use their observing self to talk back to their inner perfectionists. Some people argue with their perfectionist. This might sound something like:

- *No, I'm not a loser. I'm good at a lot of things!*

Others might believe the criticisms and give up:

- *You're right. I suck. I'll just quit now.*

Other people might take some extreme action to punish the perfectionist:

- *You want to see loser? I'll show you loser. I'll bomb this test on purpose and fail the class!*

What are the ways that you respond to your inner perfectionist voice? Do any of these patterns (arguing, giving up, acting out) feel familiar? Or is there another way you have of talking back to your voice?

look inside

Find a quiet spot where you won't be interrupted, with at least two chairs or other places to sit. Sit in one chair. Close your eyes for a moment and get in touch with your observing self, the part that sees and hears everything that happens.

Now imagine your perfectionist self is in the other chair. If it helps, review activity 23 to call to mind the way your inner perfectionist looks and sounds. Listen to what that perfectionist part has to say right now. Is your perfectionist worried about school, dating, an argument with family, or something else? Now listen to how your observing self responds. Write out the dialogue between these two parts, making sure to include what each part says and how each part feels.

Inner perfectionist says: _____

_____

Inner perfectionist feels: _____

_____

Observing self responds: _____

_____

Observing self feels: _____

_____

activity 25 ✳ how do you respond to your inner perfectionist?

Inner perfectionist responds: _____

_____

Inner perfectionist feels: _____

_____

Observing self responds: _____

_____

Observing self feels: _____

_____

dig deeper

Does this conversation sound familiar? Are there other people in your life who talk to you the way your perfectionist voice talks? Describe a situation where someone talked or acted in a way that reminds you of your perfectionist voice.

_____

_____

_____

_____

What thoughts, emotions, and sensations do you notice as you remember this?

_____

_____

Now think of some relationships in your life where things go differently. Perhaps you have a friend or family member who talks to you differently than your perfectionist voice does. Maybe someone was kind or caring, or helped you solve a problem, or perhaps distracted you in a way that made you feel better. Describe a situation like this.

_____

_____

_____

_____

How is what this person said or did different from what your perfectionist voice would have said or done?

_____

_____

How did you feel inside when this person responded in this way?

_____

_____

Is there a part inside you that might be able to respond to your inner perfectionist in this way? Maybe this part has comforted or helped a friend or family member who was self-critical or afraid or hard on himself.

Imagine responding to yourself the way you would treat a close friend. Describe what that compassionate voice would say or do.

_____

_____

_____

How do you feel as you imagine talking to yourself with kindness?

_____

_____

talking back to the voice of 26 perfectionism

consider this

When your inner perfectionist speaks up, it can be hard to hear anything else. That voice can get so loud! It's hard to talk back to that voice when the volume is all the way up to 100 percent.

The more you build awareness of that perfectionist voice as a part of you, not all of you, the easier it gets to turn the volume down. As you build some separation between your perfectionist part and your observing self, you can start to hear yourself think. Getting some distance from your perfectionist voice can also help you talk back to it in more helpful ways.

There are a lot of different ways you can respond to your inner perfectionist. Some of those involve words (using your head), some involve feelings (using your heart), and some involve doing things (taking action). In this activity, we'll explore using your head, by talking back with words or other thought-based methods of challenging perfectionism such as these:

- *Naming it.* When the perfectionist speaks, pause and label its words for what they are: judgments, insults, criticisms, fears. Remember that whatever the perfectionist is saying is only an opinion, not a fact.

- *Reviewing the evidence.* Look around and see what evidence exists to disprove the perfectionist's criticisms or predictions of disaster. What facts show that you are *not* stupid, unlikable, a failure, and so on? Have you seen other people make similar mistakes and not experience catastrophe? Review those facts in your head or write them down to counter the perfectionist's claims.

- *Exploring alternate explanations.* Your perfectionist part has one view of the situation, usually a pretty extreme one. What are some other views? Imagine another part of yourself talking, or try to see the situation through the eyes of a good friend or family member.

- *Goal-directed thinking.* What is your perfectionist voice trying to accomplish with its critical statements? Is it trying to motivate you to work harder, or spare you from being embarrassed at a party? (Review activity 24 if you need help figuring this out.) Ask yourself, *Is this the best way to reach my goal?* Make a list of other thoughts or actions that would be more productive.

- *Watching the waves.* In this method, you don't respond to the perfectionist part at all; you simply observe it talking or feeling, as you would observe waves rising and falling in the ocean. (You can review activity 21 for more details on this practice.) Don't try to ignore it or push it away, but don't argue with it or talk back to it either.

look inside

Read the following descriptions of perfectionist attacks. Each scenario has two responses. One is unproductive and keeps the person feeling bad. The other is a healthier response that stops or softens the perfectionist attack. Put a check next to each healthy reply.

Destiny gets her math homework back and cringes at the grade: B-minus. Destiny's inner perfectionist says, "You're never going to amount to anything with grades like that!"

A *You're right. I should have triple-checked my work before handing it in. I suck.*

B *Beating myself up won't help me learn. I'm going to buy myself a juice and review what I got wrong.*

Hunter really wants to impress the guy he has a crush on, and spends a long time rehearsing what he is going to say at the party. When he tries to talk to the guy, he's too shy to speak. His inner perfectionist says, "You're so socially awkward; you're hopeless."

A Hunter watches the critical thought come and go, and when it passes he tries to talk to the guy again.

B Hunter leaves the party and goes home alone, feeling hopeless.

Morgan is trying really hard to get along better with her sister but gets really frustrated and snaps at her anyway, sparking a big fight. Her inner perfectionist says, "You're an angry person! Why can't you just be nice?"

A *Whatever, I'm never going to be nicer. Why bother even trying.*

B *If my best friend were here, she'd say no one can be nice all the time, and I did the best I could on a stressful day.*

Sean gets the news that he didn't get the summer internship he wanted and is wait-listed at his top-choice college. His inner perfectionist says, "Well, it's over now. You're never going to have the life you want."

A *I can fix this. I'll appeal the decision. I'll call them and beg them to let me in. There has to be something I can do.*

B *I'm going to get a good education at my second- or third-choice school too. I asked three adults I like if they're still upset about not getting into their top college and every single person said no.*

Julia comes in third place at an important track meet. Her inner perfectionist says, "That's what you get for being lazy at practices...third place, third rate."

A *Insults. Judgments. That's your opinion, perfectionist, not a fact.*

B *It's not my fault! The coach should have made us practice in hotter weather like this, and my mom should have woken me up earlier like I asked. How am I supposed to win when everyone lets me down?*

Now go back and for each healthy reply, write in which method the person was using: *naming it, reviewing evidence, alternate explanations, goal-directed thinking,* or *watching the waves.*

Destiny: _____

Hunter: _____

Morgan: _____

Sean: _____

Julia: _____

Sometimes the first technique you try doesn't work, and the perfectionist keeps bugging you. When this happens, you can switch gears and pick a new strategy.

Practice switching gears now. For each scenario above, write out another possible healthy response. Use a different method than the example.

Destiny: _____

_____

Hunter: _____

_____

Morgan: _____

_____

Sean: _____

_____

Julia: _____

_____

dig deeper

Think of a recent time your inner perfectionist attacked you. Write down what your perfectionist said:

_____

_____

_____

Read over this perfectionist attack. Take a moment and scan your inner experience. What do you feel in your body as you read this attack?

_____

_____

What emotions do you feel?

_____

_____

What thoughts does your observing self have as the perfectionist speaks?

_____

_____

Using one of the thought-based strategies, think of a different way to respond. Write down what you want to say below. Or, if you're "watching the waves," describe your experience of observing and not responding.

_____

_____

_____

What do you feel in your body as you read this new response?

_____

Emotions? _____

Thoughts? _____

Remember, if one cognitive strategy doesn't work, switch to another, or move on to the heart-focused or action-oriented strategies in the next two activities. Not all tools work for all people, and a tool that works for you in one situation might not help in another.

27 changing your emotional response to perfectionism

consider this

Sometimes using logic, evidence, and observation just doesn't make a difference to your inner perfectionist. If you have tried talking back using head-based strategies and been met with a skeptical response from the perfectionist voice—lots of "yeah, but"s or dismissive eye rolling—you might want to try a different tactic: using your heart.

Responding with your heart means focusing on the emotions your observing self is feeling—rather than thoughts, evidence, arguments, or actions. You likely feel hurt, sad, or scared when you first hear your inner perfectionist speak. If you pause and take a breath, you might also find that you feel something else underneath. You may feel anger at the perfectionist's bullying or compassion for the perfectionist's fears and anxieties, or you may find yourself laughing a bit at the perfectionist's over-the-top beliefs. Focusing on these emotions can help you respond to your inner perfectionist in one of these heart-centered ways:

- *Humor.* Try responding to your inner perfectionist by making a joke, laughing lightly at that part's predictions of disaster or unrealistic expectations. Don't get mean-spirited with your humor—you don't want to get into a name-calling contest with your inner perfectionist!

- *Assertiveness.* Experiment with using a firm tone when replying to your perfectionist part. The words you use might be as simple as "No!" or "Stop that!" The words are not as important as the energy you put behind them. Assertiveness comes from a sense of strength, standing up for yourself, and feeling confident that you deserve respect instead of the criticism your inner perfectionist delivers.

- *Compassion.* As you may remember from activity 24, your inner perfectionist is usually acting from a sense of fear that something terrible is going to happen if you're not perfect. If you picture your perfectionist part as a scared little kid, you may notice feelings of caring and compassion arising. Try responding to your inner perfectionist with a loving tone, offering reassurance that things will be okay even if you don't perform perfectly.

look inside

Talking to yourself with compassion, strength, or kind and gentle humor might be really new and unfamiliar. It may be hard to even imagine how you can do it, what you would say, how you would sound.

You might be more familiar with other people in your life talking to you in these heart-centered ways. Think of times friends, parents, teachers, or others treated you with kindness and love, stood up for you, or used humor in a gentle and sweet way to help you feel better about yourself. In each column below, write down examples from your life.

Compassion	Assertiveness	Humor

dig deeper

Pick one example from each column above. Think back to how you felt when you got that response. Write down the thoughts, feelings, and body sensations you remember.

Compassionate response: _____

_____

_____

Assertive response: _____

_____

_____

Humorous response: _____

_____

_____

Now imagine giving those same responses to yourself. What is it like to take in the kindness or strength you're offering yourself?

_____

_____

_____

_____

28 standing up to your perfectionism

consider this

When your inner perfectionist is shouting at you, you can respond with your head or your heart. You can also stand up to it by taking action. This could mean:

- *Exercising.* Vigorous exercise can tire you out, which means less energy available to the perfectionist. Exercise also releases endorphins, which are your body's natural mood-lifters. When you're feeling more positive overall, it's harder for the inner perfectionist to shout so loud.

- *Soothing.* Sometimes a calming, loving action might be better than vigorous exercise. Soothing action could mean taking a bath, meditating, praying, or wrapping your arms around yourself in a hug. Or maybe asking someone you trust for a hug!

- *Distracting.* When your inner perfectionist is criticizing you, try briefly acknowledging that voice, and then turning your attention to something really interesting. Watch a favorite movie, get absorbed in a book, talk to good friends—whatever will capture your attention.

- *Experimenting.* If your inner perfectionist is worried or predicting catastrophe, try conducting an experiment to see how true those thoughts are. For example, if your perfectionist thinks going to the party without looking perfect will be a disaster, try going in a less-than-perfect outfit and pay attention to what happens.

look inside

Think of three ways you could use exercise to reply to your inner perfectionist. These could be brief moments of movement or full-on workouts.

1. _____

2. _____

3. _____

What about soothing? Imagine three ways you could respond with kindness. You might think of words or actions, or just describe the tone you could use.

1. _____

2. _____

3. _____

Imagine three ways you could distract yourself from an inner-perfectionist attack.

1. _____

2. _____

3. _____

And write down three experiments you could create to challenge your inner perfectionist.

1. _____

2. _____

3. _____

Choose one of these ideas and put it into action this week. Write down what happens below.

Briefly describe the inner perfectionist attack:

_____

_____

How did you respond?

_____

_____

What did you feel afterwards? What thoughts, emotions, or body sensations did you notice?

_____

_____

_____

dig deeper

Practicing physical responses to your inner perfectionist might make you increasingly aware of the physical pains you feel as a result of perfectionist stress, criticism, and anxiety. You may be noticing muscle tension, headaches, or other aches you didn't pay attention to before, or didn't connect to your struggle with perfectionism. Progressive muscle relaxation is a tool that can help you relax and release muscles so you can reduce the physical pain from stress and anxiety. You might also find that a few minutes of this technique quiets down an inner perfectionist attack!

Progressive Muscle Relaxation

You'll need about five minutes for this exercise. Sit in a comfortable chair and take off your shoes. Silence your phone and other devices. Start by focusing on your breath for five cycles of inhaling and exhaling. Bring your attention to your body, and notice any aches, pains, or tension.

Now focus on the top part of your head and face. Squeeze all the muscles around your forehead and eyes, and hold for five seconds. Now let go, and for ten seconds, *really* pay attention to the feeling of relaxation in that part of your body. Try exhaling as you let go, and picture the tightness and pain flowing out of your muscles like water going down a drain. Next clench your jaw and mouth, and release. Work your way down your body, alternately clenching each muscle group for five seconds and relaxing for ten. Really drink in the feeling of relaxation in each muscle group!

Muscle Groups

Forehead and eyes	Right arm
Jaw	Right hand
Neck and shoulders	(Repeat on other side)
Chest	Right thigh
Stomach	Right lower leg
Back	Right foot
Buttocks	(Repeat on other side)

When you're finished, take another five breaths in and out, and scan your body again. Do you feel any different than you did when you started? Write down any changes you notice in thoughts, feelings, or sensations.

_____

_____

_____

how to stop comparing 29
yourself to others

consider this

Even if you meet your own incredibly high standards, when someone else appears to be doing "better" than you it can send you into a tailspin. You start comparing yourself to others and end up feeling less-than, dejected, depressed. Or maybe comparing yourself to others results in your feeling angry and jealous, causing damage to your friendships.

Competition is unavoidable, especially for young people. Sports often have winners and losers; scholarships and prizes are awarded to only a few people who try for them; a job is given to one applicant out of a pool of many. You may even feel like you're competing with friends or siblings for love, attention, or approval.

Competition can bring up unhealthy thoughts, feelings, and actions, but there are also healthy ways to compete. Check out the chart below to see examples of each. Do you recognize any warning signs of unhealthy competition in your thoughts, feelings, and actions?

Unhealthy Competition	Healthy Competition
Engaging in all-or-nothing thinking: one person winning means other people losing, one person being smart means others are dumb	Participating in activities that allow lots of people to succeed, rather than one winner and many losers
Insulting or gossiping about other people who do "better" than you as a way to make yourself feel better about "losing"	Appreciating others' skills and strengths; asking for help or advice from others who are doing well
Having difficulty feeling happy for other people who do well, because all you can think about are the ways you don't measure up	Feeling genuinely happy for others' successes
Losing friends because you're angry or jealous about their successes	Accepting your feelings of envy or disappointment without acting on them
Mistrusting peers or looking for ways to sabotage them because you're afraid they're out to hurt you	Looking to friends for support when things are hard, and to share joy in good times
Withdrawing from relationships when you aren't doing well, because you don't feel worthy	Finding ways to support, collaborate, and work with friends so that you all learn and succeed

look inside

You can't always control your initial response to competition. In a competitive environment, you may have negative thoughts or intense feelings of jealousy. This is normal! The important thing is what you do next. How do you respond to your inner perfectionist and to other people, and where do those responses take you?

Read each scenario and, using one color pen or pencil, draw a line from the initial situation to the unhealthy choices that follow. Use a different color to trace the path of healthy choices.

Angela loses a tennis match to her good friend

Feels disappointed, and also proud of her friend

Compares herself to her friend; feels jealous

Congratulates her friend, even though she feels a bit jealous too

Friend is happy and grateful; shares practice tips with Angela

Looks for ways her friend might have cheated

Spreads rumors about her friend cheating

Friendship strengthens, and Angela wins the next match

Friendship ends

Marisol gets a B on her paper; her friend gets an A

Feels disappointed and worries her friend thinks less of her now

Feels upset, but believes she can improve

Asks friend if they can read each other's papers

Feels inspired by her friend's writing

Calls her friend smart; criticizes and beats herself up

Withdraws from friendship

Cancels study dates with friend because she's embarrassed

Feels closer to her friend and more confident in her writing

Brendan wants top score on a test

Channels anxiety into forming a study group

Worries his friends will do better than he will

Shares what he knows with his friends and gets tips for himself

Distracts his friends with texts when they're studying

Doesn't share knowledge or tips when his friends ask for help

Brendan and a few friends all get 100 percent on the test

Group celebrates together; friendships strengthen

Feels guilty when he does better than his friends, and avoids them for a week

dig deeper

Competitive urges, thoughts of comparison, and feelings of envy are natural and happen to everyone. Describe a recent time you compared yourself to someone else, felt jealous, or had an intense desire to win.

_____

_____

What thoughts and emotions did your perfectionist part have about you in this situation?

_____

_____

What thoughts and emotions did your perfectionist part have about the other person or people involved?

_____

_____

Remember that the thoughts and emotions you're feeling are normal. You can't stop yourself from feeling a certain way, but you can choose how to respond to your inner perfectionist or to the other people involved.

What are healthy and unhealthy choices you can make in response to these emotions and thoughts? What might happen next?

Unhealthy action: _____

_____

What happens next? _____

_____

Healthy action: _____

_____

What happens next? _____

_____

Does it feel difficult or painful to choose the healthy option? What might get in the way? Describe the obstacles that might prevent you from making healthy choices.

_____

_____

_____

how to have realistic 30
expectations of others

consider this

It's good to have high standards in relationships, to expect to be treated with respect and kindness by friends, family, romantic partners, and others. It shows that you value yourself and know you deserve to be treated well. However, sometimes people with perfectionist traits turn high standards into impossible standards and start expecting perfection from the other people in their lives.

Of course, it's impossible for other people to be perfect, just like it's impossible for you to be perfect. People make mistakes, forget things, and have bad days. You might feel hurt, angry, or disappointed as a result, and feel a little break or crack in your relationship with that person. In healthy relationships, both people can acknowledge their feelings, talk to each other, repair the break, and move on.

When you have unhealthy, unrealistic expectations of others, it can be really hard to talk about your feelings and make those repairs. Here are some common experiences of people who expect perfection from others:

- strong feelings of anger and hurt, even at small mistakes

- criticizing or complaining about others

- difficulty having empathy or seeing things from others' perspectives

- finding it very difficult to forgive others and move on

- feeling guarded, having a hard time trusting others or feeling close

look inside

Olivia is captain of the softball team. She really wants to have a successful season. When her teammate Amanda makes a good play or scores a run, Olivia shouts enthusiastic praise. When Amanda strikes out or misses a catch, Olivia gets really frustrated and usually yells something critical ("What's wrong with you! How could you miss that?") or disappointed ("You have to do better than that!").

How do you imagine Olivia is feeling? _____

How do you imagine Amanda is feeling? _____

What are some possible reasons Amanda might make a mistake in a game or practice?

_____

What are Olivia's expectations of Amanda? _____

_____

Circle the unrealistic expectations. What might be more realistic expectations of her teammate? Write some ideas below.

_____

_____

_____

Chloe has been dating Kyle for a couple of months. She really likes him and enjoys herself when they spend time together. When they can't see each other in person, Chloe expects Kyle to text her throughout the evening. She feels really hurt when he forgets, and she's guarded and withdrawn around him for days afterward.

How do you imagine Chloe is feeling? _____

How do you imagine Kyle is feeling? _____

What are some possible reasons Kyle might be out of touch? _____

_____

What are Chloe's expectations of Kyle? _____

Circle the unrealistic expectations. What might be more realistic expectations?

_____

_____

_____

Can you think of times in your life when you felt strongly angry or disappointed in another person? Describe one situation in the space below.

_____

_____

_____

What were your expectations of the other person in this situation?

_____

_____

What expectations were realistic?

_____

_____

What expectations were unrealistic?

_____

_____

dig deeper

Having realistic expectations of others does not prevent you from ever feeling hurt, disappointed, or angry. All relationships involve mistakes or hurt feelings at some point, and acknowledging those wounds and repairing them is an important part in building strong relationships. In activity 15, you learned how to make healthy apologies; how you accept an apology from others is just as important. Here are some things to keep in mind when someone is apologizing to you:

- *Does it sound and feel like a healthy apology?* Check in with your emotions; does the apology *feel* sincere? Do you hear regret, responsibility, and remedy?

- *If it doesn't feel sincere, keep talking.* Say more about how the person's actions impacted you, and what you need for remedy or repair. You don't have to say, "That's okay" when you don't feel that way!

- *If it feels genuine, accept it.* Acknowledge your friend's efforts by saying, "I accept your apology" or "Thank you for apologizing."

- *An apology is a first step.* Sometimes it's all that's needed, but other times you might need more repair before you can forgive. It's okay to say, "Although I accept your apology, I'm not quite ready to forgive yet. Let's keep talking about it and working on rebuilding trust."

- *What if no apology is coming?* If you feel hurt and your friend isn't apologizing, try stating what the person did and how it made you feel: "When you yelled at me in practice, I felt hurt and angry."

Describe a recent time someone apologized to you.

_____

_____

_____

What aspects of the apology were healthy? Check in with yourself—what words or actions made you feel better?

_____

_____

What aspects of the apology were unhealthy, or did not make you feel better?

_____

_____

Are there other words or actions you need from the other person to make the apology more meaningful, or help you move on?

_____

_____

consider this

Pressure to succeed can come from all directions—parents, friends, teachers, and the culture at large. Here are some of the ways you might feel pressured by others:

- You get compared to a successful sibling or peer.

- Someone expresses disappointment with your less-than-perfect performance.

- You get punished (for example, you lose a spot on a team or lose privileges at home) for good—but not perfect—grades or scores.

- It seems the only attention or praise you get is for perfect grades.

- You assume others expect perfection from you, because that's what you expect from yourself.

The person delivering the message may or may not be intending to pressure you—it's not always easy to tell. Either way, you feel stressed, worried, and on edge. This is especially true when the pressure is coming from someone important to you. You can start to feel like any drop in your performance is going to be the cause of someone else's sadness, anger, or disappointment.

The truth is you can't be responsible for anyone else's happiness or sense of satisfaction. You can only do your best, and you deserve love and appreciation regardless of the outcome of a race, test, class, or contest.

look inside

The first step to reducing feelings of stress and pressure from other people is to identify those messages as you hear them. Think about each category of life listed below, and write down any messages you have received that felt like pressure to be perfect. These might be things people said or did, things they didn't say, or situations you observed.

Family: _____

_____

School: _____

_____

Sports or activities: _____

_____

Friends: _____

_____

Dating: _____

_____

Other (for example, religious community or neighbors): _____

_____

What messages are others sending you about performance and perfection? List them on the left side of the paper. What different, healthier, more realistic expectations do you (or could you) have about yourself? List them on the right.

Other People's Messages	Healthier Expectations
_____	_____
_____	_____
_____	_____
_____	_____

Imagine a boundary between other people's messages of pressure and your own more healthy expectations of self. To *really* protect you, how thick does it need to be? What color feels right? Does it need to have a different texture in certain places to block really painful messages?

Now draw the boundary you imagined, a boundary that shields you from the unhealthy, unrealistic messages, keeps you safe, and gives you space to take in your own healthy messages.

Other People's
Messages

Healthier
Expectations

dig deeper

When you feel pressure from family, friends, teachers, or others, try envisioning the line you drew here. Close your eyes if you can, take a few deep breaths, and picture its color, texture, and thickness. Picture whatever messages the person is delivering bouncing off the boundary and staying on its side. Visualize your healthy messages staying close to you, really getting in.

Did picturing your boundary help? Describe your experience here.

_____

_____

_____

avoiding the avoidance trap 32

consider this

When you feel anxious about something, it's natural to want to avoid it. Avoiding gives you a moment of relief—you don't have to face the scary thing! That feels good for a minute, but in the long run avoidance actually *increases* your anxiety. You start to believe that the scary thing is truly dangerous and that you can't handle it. And the next time you face it—the test, the party, whatever is making you worried—you get even more anxious because of that belief. Avoidance traps you in a vicious cycle, with your anxiety getting worse every time.

Avoidance can also impact your life in other ways. If you turn down social invitations or don't show up when you said you would, friends may stop asking you to do things. If you avoid tests, your grades may suffer; skipping games and performances can also have consequences.

The way out of the avoidance trap is to feel your anxiety and *do the scary thing anyway.* That might sound really hard, but if you go slowly and take it step by step, you can break the cycle.

look inside

Avoidance can take many forms. Check out the list of actions and behaviors below. Circle any that you use. Use the blank lines to write in any other ways you avoid.

Not answering the phone

Blowing off homework or studying

Skipping games or performances

Turning down invitations to hang out

Saying yes to invitations, then not going

Not trying new activities, sports, subjects

_____

_____

Which of these habits would you most like to change? Choose three specific goals you would like to work toward. Write your goals in positive language (what you would like to increase) rather than negative language (what you would like to decrease). For example, if you would like to change your habit of turning down invitations, your goal might be to go out with friends one night per week.

1. _____

2. _____

3. _____

dig deeper

To break out of the avoidance trap, develop a step-by-step plan to face your anxiety head-on. Check out these stories to see how other people have challenged their urge to avoid.

> *Jenny feels anxious about social interactions. Her inner perfectionist tells her she can't go out with friends unless she looks perfect, knows the right things to say, and is in a perfectly good mood. That part believes if any of those things are off, Jenny will embarrass herself and then no one will like her. Whenever Jenny gets a text inviting her to do something, her anxiety spikes and she turns her phone off. Jenny feels some relief in the moment, but she's been noticing her friends are drifting away.*

Jenny's goal: Go out with group of friends for an hour

Jenny's plan:

1. Imagine going out with her friends.

2. Have a text conversation with one friend.

3. Have a group text conversation.

4. Go out with one friend for coffee.

5. Go out with two friends for an hour.

6. See a group of friends for five minutes—plan to run into them at the mall when she's on her way to something else.

7. Go out with a group of friends for an hour.

Deven gets super nervous about taking tests. His inner perfectionist wants him to get 100 percent on everything, and the possibility of making a mistake makes his heart race and his brain freeze. Deven has skipped several algebra classes to avoid taking tests, and as a result he's in danger of failing.

Deven's goal: Take a test in algebra class

Deven's plan:

1. While at home, imagine taking a test in school.

2. Study with a friend, and use flashcards to practice answering questions.

3. Take a practice test at home with no timer.

4. Take a practice test at home with a timer set to the length of a class period.

5. During some downtime in algebra class, spend a couple of minutes vividly imagining taking a test.

6. Take a short practice quiz in his algebra classroom after school or during a free period.

7. Take a real test in algebra class.

To create your own plan for breaking an avoidance trap, pick one of the goals from your previous list. Write out some steps that lead up to your ultimate goal. For now, don't worry about the order; just write down a range of steps you could take, from right outside your comfort zone to almost as hard as the final goal.

_____

_____

_____

_____

_____

_____

Look through your steps and rank them in order from least to most challenging. Use Jenny's and Deven's examples as a guide. If all the steps seem too hard or too easy, go back and revise your list so that each step is only a little harder than the one before. Once the steps are in order, you have a plan to break one of your avoidance traps!

Next, it's time to take the first step. It's normal to feel anxiety before and during—it's really important to face your anxiety head on, breathe, and keep going! Repeat the first step several times, until you feel little or no anxiety. Then move on to the next step. When you get through the whole list and achieve your goal, take a moment to celebrate. You broke out of the avoidance trap! When you're ready, make a plan for the next anxiety-provoking goal on your list.

If your anxiety stays the same or increases after several repetitions, you may need to slow down and take smaller steps. You can make steps smaller by changing any or all of these:

- the length of time you're trying something

- the location or time of day of the step

- the people with you as you take the step

You can also share the steps you created with a counselor to get some help coming up with a new plan.

33 don't take it personally

consider this

Zoe feels really nervous any time she is the center of attention—giving a speech, talking in a group of friends, and especially when playing a violin solo in a concert. Her inner perfectionist believes that other people notice every flat note she plays. She sees some people in the audience looking at their phones, and she assumes they're making negative comments about her on social media. Tears well up in her eyes, and she starts feeling really down about herself.

Juan gets super anxious when talking to teachers, coaches, friends' parents, or almost any adult. When he talks with his math teacher, his inner perfectionist starts whispering in his head, telling him he's not making any sense. Juan's anxiety gets so intense that he can't think very well. He feels a lump in his throat, and he can barely get words out. He sees his teacher looking at him quietly, waiting. Juan believes the teacher thinks he's stupid.

Whenever she hangs out with friends, Aubrey feels intensely self-conscious. Her inner perfectionist works so hard to think of the perfect thing to say or the perfect way to look that Aubrey can't relax and enjoy herself. Her friends invite her out on Friday night; Aubrey spends a lot of time planning her clothes, redoing her makeup, and rehearsing things to say, but it never feels good enough. Her heart starts racing, her breath gets fast, and she starts to feel panic. She blows off her friends and stays home alone. Her friends text her asking her where she is and telling her they really want to see her, but she thinks they're being insincere.

Zoe, Juan, and Aubrey all believe they know how others are seeing them and what they're thinking. They believe the people around them notice every flaw and judge every misstep. This is called the *spotlight effect*. Researchers have found that people drastically overestimate how much others notice them, especially when they've done something they feel is embarrassing.

The truth is, most people aren't watching others that closely and don't remember or judge every mistake. In reality, we're all wrapped up in our own thoughts and problems, and each of us is our own worst critic. The people you think are noticing you are most likely thinking about themselves and worried about what you're thinking of them!

If Zoe, Juan, and Aubrey could actually see what was inside the heads of the people in their lives, they would learn this:

- Most of the people in the audience at Zoe's concert thought her solo was great. A few who weren't that into music were distracted by their phones and had no negative thoughts about Zoe at all.

- Juan's math teacher feels very patient as he listens to Juan and remembers how hard it was for him to talk to adults when he was a kid.

- Aubrey's friends really do want her to come hang out. They enjoy her company—especially when she's relaxed and spontaneous. They don't notice the little things Aubrey is so self-conscious about, partly because they're focused on themselves and how they look and act.

look inside

Zoe, Juan, and Aubrey's anxieties stem from the distorted thoughts of their inner perfectionists. Can you identify the incorrect, exaggerated, or worried thoughts they each had?

Zoe: _____

Juan: _____

Aubrey: _____

Zoe, Juan, and Aubrey also felt emotions when their inner perfectionists spoke up. What were the feelings each of them had when their anxiety started?

Zoe: _____

Juan: _____

Aubrey: _____

In addition to thoughts and emotions, they each felt some physical changes when their inner perfectionists spoke up. What physical sensations did each of them feel?

Zoe: _____

Juan: _____

Aubrey: _____

dig deeper

Think about times in your life when you felt anxious about a social situation—maybe when you were hanging out with friends, dating, performing, or speaking in public. Describe one situation here:

_____

_____

_____

What were the thoughts you had during this situation?

_____

_____

Circle the thoughts that were distorted.

What emotions did you feel?

_____

_____

Circle the feelings that came as a result of your inner perfectionist making you anxious.

What physical sensations did you experience?

_____

_____

Circle the ones that were linked to your anxiety.

activity 33 * don't take it personally

Look at the distorted thoughts you circled. What are alternate explanations for them?

_____

_____

_____

consider this

Wanting to do well in your daily activities, wanting to be good to others you care about, aiming to achieve great things in life—these are all wonderful qualities in a person. However, all these big goals and ambitions can get a little overwhelming. It can be hard to know where to start, and the pressure to do well on really important things can feel paralyzing. Your inner perfectionist can whisper all sorts of things in your ear: you aren't ready to get started, the project is too hard, you can do it later.

That voice can make you anxious and afraid, and you may find yourself trying to get rid of those uncomfortable thoughts and feelings by avoiding getting started or putting off finishing to the last minute. Procrastination is a form of self-handicapping—creating obstacles so that you have a ready-made excuse if you don't perform well. "Of course my paper was terrible. I wrote it in three hours!"

Procrastination can get in the way of getting what you want and also can make you feel pretty terrible about yourself. If doing things well is an important part of who you are, it can be pretty distressing to have the process of doing the work be so tortured.

look inside

What are the things you do when you're procrastinating? Maybe you talk to friends, watch videos, check social media, sleep, or eat. Or perhaps you engage in endless research and organizing to prepare yourself to get started…only you never seem to actually start. We all have our go-to procrastination activities. List yours below:

_____

_____

_____

When you notice yourself engaging in these activities, pause and ask yourself, *Am I doing this because I want to or need to? Or am I doing it to avoid another task that is overwhelming me?*

If you're engaging in avoidance or procrastination, check in to see what role your inner perfectionist is playing in this situation. Is that part of you worrying that you aren't ready or that your work won't be good enough? Or maybe something else?

_____

_____

What emotions and physical sensations did you notice as your inner perfectionist was speaking and you were procrastinating?

_____

_____

dig deeper

When you notice you're engaged in procrastination, you can try one of the following techniques to get yourself back on track:

- *Learn to manage time differently.* If you have an hour or longer of work to do, it can feel overwhelming to get started. Try breaking your time down into more manageable chunks. Make a commitment to work for a short period of time; start with fifteen minutes. Clear your workspace, turn off your phone and other distractions, and set a timer. If you feel the pull of checking your social media or getting up for a snack or anything else, wait until the timer goes off. Then set yourself a timer for a break for three minutes, and let yourself do whatever you want during that time. Then it's back to work for another fifteen! Experiment with different lengths of work and break time to find the right rhythm for you.

- *Make tasks less painful or boring.* If you're avoiding something because it's really unpleasant, take a few minutes to think creatively. Can you change an assignment to make it more fun? Can you add something pleasant to an otherwise dull task, like listening to music during exercise?

- *Take the pressure off.* Are you getting stuck in perfectionist thinking, believing you have to do this task perfectly? What are the actual consequences if you get less than 100 percent on this test? Are the stakes as high as your inner perfectionist fears?

- *Get rid of distractions.* Silence your phone, close any browser tabs you don't need, and turn off all messaging apps. Make sure food, friends, music, and other temptations are out of reach while you get work done.

- *Get a little help from a friend.* Make your intention or deadline public, or at least known to one or two other people who will help you stay accountable.

Which of the methods did you try when facing procrastination?

_____

Did the method help you get started or get back to work faster than usual? Why do you think it helped or didn't help?

_____

_____

What changes, if any, did you notice in what your inner perfectionist was saying, or how you were feeling, after trying this method?

_____

_____

_____

consider this

Perfectionists often want to be perfect at *everything*. Of course, this is impossible, and leaves you feeling disappointed or angry at yourself a lot of the time. Setting goals can help you focus on what really matters to you, rather than feeling overwhelmed by the pressure to do everything and do it perfectly. Goals also help you stay on track, so you can feel more confident and optimistic that you're doing well. They give you opportunities to feel proud of yourself for taking steps along the way.

What are the aspects of healthy goal setting?

- *Set attainable goals.* If you have a full load of classes and a part-time job, aiming to also write a novel in a month is not realistic. Similarly, if you hate running, you aren't setting yourself up for success by striving to win a marathon.

- *Break your goal down into manageable steps.* Break down your ultimate goal into smaller, short-term steps. This helps you know where to get started and what to do next, and gives you a sense of making progress even when your long-term goal is still far in the distance. You can also celebrate milestones along the way!

- *Set realistic deadlines.* When you don't have a deadline, it's easy to put off getting started. As a result, sometimes you never make progress on something you really want to achieve. Setting realistic deadlines means giving yourself enough time to actually complete each step, but not so much that you lose focus and get distracted.

- *Gauge progress by measurable markers.* If your goal is to get an A in your history class, and the steps along the way include getting 90 percent or higher on the midterm and final, it's easy to gauge your progress. If your goal is to be a better big sister, it's harder to find measurable markers for success along the way. Try setting concrete steps for yourself, like "Invite your little sister to a one-on-one activity once a week," or "Say thanks sincerely when your sister does one of your chores for you."

look inside

Think of a goal you have right now, in any area of your life: school, work, relationships, sports, or others. Pick one that feels hard but not overwhelming. For this exercise, choose a short-term goal—one you can accomplish in a few days or two weeks at the most.

Goal: _____

Manageable steps: Use the space below to break down the steps to achieving your goal. Don't worry about getting them in order at first. Just write them down, and when you're done, go back and number them in the order you're going to tackle them.

_____

_____

_____

_____

_____

_____

Deadlines: Once you have put your steps in order, set deadlines for each one. Remember to be realistic about your timeframe. Think about what else is going on in your life, and give yourself enough time to get things done. Write your deadline next to the step in your list above.

Measurable markers: How will you know when you've completed each step? Make sure you're setting reasonable markers for yourself, and not expecting perfection for every step. Write in a marker for each step here.

_____

_____

_____

_____

_____

Put it all together: Fill in this outline with the information you just wrote down. If you have more steps or need more space, write your outline down on another piece of paper. You're ready to get started on your goals!

Goal: _____

Step 1: _____

Deadline: _____

Marker: _____

Step 2: _____

Deadline: _____

Marker: _____

Step 3: _____

Deadline: _____

Marker: _____

Step 4: _____

Deadline: _____

Marker: _____

Step 5: _____

Deadline: _____

Marker: _____

When you've accomplished your goal, congratulate yourself! Then come back to this page and write down the date and outcome.

_____

_____

dig deeper

How did you feel as you were working toward this goal? Did you notice any difference from other times when you did not map out a goal with detailed steps?

_____

_____

_____

Do you think you would have accomplished this goal without a plan? If so, would it have taken you the same amount of time, less, or more?

_____

What was it like to accomplish each step along the way? Did you feel any pride, happiness, or relief as you completed each step? If not, what got in the way?

_____

_____

36 it's okay to ask for help

consider this

Perfectionists often find it really tough to ask for help. That voice inside tells you that admitting you can't do something all by yourself is a sign of weakness, or that getting help will make you a burden on others. Or maybe your inner perfectionist is telling you that no one else will do it correctly, so you have to do it yourself if you want it done right.

The truth is, asking for help is not a sign of weakness, it's actually a sign of strength. Asking for help requires self-awareness, honesty, and vulnerability—and those qualities don't come easy! Your inner perfectionist doesn't want you to do it all alone because it makes you stronger; it wants you to go it alone because it's afraid of rejection or ridicule. Facing those fears and asking anyway requires a lot of courage.

What's the point in summoning up the courage and strength to ask for help, you may wonder. It's so hard and scary, why *not* just do it all alone and save yourself the trouble and risk? When you ask for help, you gain these advantages:

- *A new perspective.* Getting an outside view on your problem can help you think about things in a new way, or find creative solutions by working with someone.

- *An opportunity to learn.* A friend or teacher may have a tool or technique that is new to you.

- *A chance to connect.* Rather than feeling burdened, most people feel pleased to be asked for help and enjoy supporting their friends. Research shows that both the helper and the helped feel closer to each other after an act of giving.

look inside

Think of a recent time you were struggling with a problem or feeling stuck in a dilemma, a time you could have asked for help but didn't. Describe the situation.

_____

_____

_____

What did your inner perfectionist say or do to talk you out of asking for help? Write down the thoughts, beliefs, and criticisms you heard from that part.

_____

_____

_____

What emotions do you feel as you imagine asking for help? _____

_____

What physical sensations? _____

_____

What is your inner perfectionist trying to accomplish by making you do this all by yourself? What is that part trying to protect you from or prove?

_____

_____

_____

dig deeper

There are ways to ask for help that can increase your self-esteem and bring other people closer to you, and there are ways that can make you feel bad about yourself and push people away. Healthy ways of seeking support involve being honest and real, not overly critical of yourself, and not offering over-the-top praise for friends (which can come across as insincere). Read through the following scenarios to learn more about how to ask for help in ways that are healthy and productive.

You need help on your calculus homework, and you approach Sharon to ask.

A "I'm so stupid, I can't figure this out. I'm going to fail!" (Then wait and hope she'll offer to help.)

B "Usually I do okay with math, but I am really struggling with this chapter. I saw you got 100 percent on the test. Can you help me?"

How do you feel as you read A? _____

How do you feel as you read B? _____

Put yourself in Sharon's shoes. How do you imagine she feels hearing each response?

A: _____

B: _____

You're struggling with your creative writing assignment. You approach your classmate Yoshi with one of these statements:

A "I admire your creative writing skills. That poem you read in class was funny and sad. Do you have time to read some of my work and give me pointers?"

B "You're such an amazing writer; you're like the best in the school. I suck so bad. I wish I could write like you."

How do you feel as you read A? _____

How do you feel as you read B? _____

How do you imagine Yoshi feels hearing each response?

A: _____

B: _____

You ask for Seth's help with feeling more comfortable in social situations. When Seth gives some suggestions of things that have worked for him, you say:

A "I can't do that. I'm not good enough at talking to people to pull it off. It won't work."

B "That sounds hard, and I'm a little skeptical it'll work, but I'll give it a try. I'm open to new ideas."

How do you feel as you read A? _____

How do you feel as you read B? _____

How do you imagine Seth feels hearing each response?

A: _____

B: _____

If you find it difficult to imagine how each helping friend would feel, conduct your own experiments in helping others. Find a few opportunities to give support, assistance, or advice to someone *who wants your help*. Notice how you feel in each situation. Do you feel burdened by your friend or critical of your friend for wanting help? Do you enjoy supporting your friend? Describe how helping feels to you.

_____

_____

_____

consider this

Perfectionism can be the cause of problems and stress, and it can also be a source of strength. People with healthy perfectionist traits often feel less anxious and more satisfied than people in general, and have strong self-esteem. Check out this list of positive perfectionist traits and see if you recognize any in yourself:

- *High (but not impossibly high!) standards.* You push yourself toward greatness, and you expect to be treated well by others.

- *Strong work ethic.* You have drive and persistence to get things done.

- *Conscientious attitude.* You believe doing good work and treating others well is the right thing to do.

- *Detail oriented.* You're focused and disciplined, catch little mistakes, and do a thorough job.

- *Organized.* You're good at putting complicated things in order, planning busy events, and strategizing on how to achieve difficult goals.

As you work on changing unhealthy aspects of perfectionism, it's also important to notice your strengths. Celebrating the healthy aspects of your perfectionism gives you much-needed opportunities for feeling good about yourself!

look inside

What positive aspects of perfectionism do you see in yourself? Look at the list above for inspiration. In the first column, write down all the qualities you like about yourself that feel connected to your perfectionism. In the next column, write down the areas of life where those qualities benefit you. In the last column, describe how each strength helps you.

Strength	Area of Life	How This Strength Helps Me
Example: Super organized	1. Homework 2. Volleyball team captain	1. Create realistic schedules for myself 2. Keep a million things in order!

dig deeper

Perfectionists tend to focus on flaws and things they want to improve and often skip out on celebrating the positive. Make a commitment to appreciate your strengths for the next week. Choose one area of life from your chart above, and each time you engage in that activity, remember your intention to appreciate your strength and skill.

To help you remember this commitment, create a physical reminder to carry with you during the activity. Check out this list for some ideas, and circle one that you'd like to use:

- a rubber band on your wrist

- an alarm or reminder on your phone

- a small rock in your pocket, maybe with a word written on it

- a necklace or other piece of jewelry with special significance

- a message written on your arm

Write your own idea here: _____

How did it go? Was it difficult to remember your strength? Did your inner perfectionist try to talk you out of feeling good about yourself?

_____

_____

_____

What positive feelings did you experience when you focused on your strengths?

_____

_____

_____

38 pulling it together

consider this

People with perfectionist personality traits can have a hard time with the messy, imperfect process of change. Your inner perfectionist might beat you up for small mistakes or setbacks, or get anxious when there isn't a clear path to success. That part may think there is a "right" or a "perfect" way to change. You can find yourself being a perfectionist about healing your perfectionism!

The truth is, change doesn't happen easily, fast, or in a straightforward way. You take two steps forward and one step back. You stall for a while and nothing seems to happen. Some things you do to change have a huge impact, and others barely inch you forward toward your goals. Even though you're making progress overall, these rough moments can make you lose faith, can trick you into thinking you're failing because things aren't going "perfectly."

As long as you're trying, you're succeeding. The bumps in the road are not only unavoidable, they can be beneficial. Mistakes, the windy road, the imperfect and unpredictable outcomes—those are the things that make you unique and interesting. Rather than avoid or hide them, you can be curious and even grateful for setbacks, seeing them as opportunities to learn, grow, get creative, and build resilience.

look inside

Think back on the activities you have done in this book. Most likely, there have been exercises where you experienced setbacks or felt that nothing was working despite your sincere effort. Describe at least three situations here.

_____

_____

_____

_____

_____

_____

Now think about some activities from this book that have had good outcomes. These can be small successes or big accomplishments. Describe at least three here.

_____

_____

_____

_____

_____

_____

Imagine each accomplishment and setback is a dot on this timeline. The setbacks go below the center line—the farther away from the line, the bigger the setback. The accomplishments go above the line—the farther away from the line, the bigger the accomplishment. Make the dots in chronological order, the order in which each happened. Write one- or two-word labels for each dot.

Now connect the dots to see a visual representation of your process of changing your perfectionism. What is it like to notice the crooked, bumpy path of change?

_____

_____

_____

Look over what you've written so far in this activity, your successes and your setbacks. You've come so far! Take a moment now to really soak in how much work you've done and how much progress you've made.

dig deeper

There may be times in the future where you forget about these successes or lose faith in your ability to move forward on your goals. For this last activity, you'll create a "perfectionist toolkit" you can take with you. This is something you can look at during those moments where you're really struggling, to help you remember the most important things you learned from this book.

Spend a few minutes sitting with each of the following questions before answering. Flip back through the book to remind yourself of what you've learned as you've wrestled with your perfectionism.

Which of these concepts were the most relevant to you or had the biggest impact? You can use the blank lines to add your own ideas. What do you want to remember about those concepts? On the page titled "My Perfectionism Toolkit," write down three to five ideas and what's important about them.

Healthy and unhealthy perfectionism	Negativity bias
The avoidance trap	Internal working model
Messages from family, school, culture	The spotlight effect
Self-esteem	Mindfulness
Vulnerability	The inner perfectionist
Superstitious beliefs	Talking back to your perfectionist
It's okay to make mistakes	Your perfectionist part is trying to help
Healthy pride versus arrogance	_____
Giving and receiving apologies	_____
Compassionate coaching	_____

Think back to all the techniques and tools you learned in this book. Did you like talking back to your inner perfectionist in a certain way? Was there a breathing exercise, a drawing or collage activity, or an experiment that helped change your experience of your perfectionism? List three to five tools and a short description of each.

Is there anything else about your unique struggle with perfectionism you want to remember? Write down any insights, hints, or thoughts you want to remember.

Finally, write a letter to your future self. Imagine a time—days, weeks, months from now—when you're feeling overwhelmed by your perfectionist thoughts or emotions and could use some encouragement. What do you think you will need to hear in that moment? What will help your anxious future self remember the pride and confidence you're feeling right now as you think about all you've learned and accomplished? Use words, drawings, or collage images—whatever speaks to you.

my perfectionism toolkit

Concepts that are important to me:

Concept: _____

Importance to me: _____

_____

Concept: _____

Importance to me: _____

_____

Concept: _____

Importance to me: _____

_____

Concept: _____

Importance to me: _____

_____

Concept: _____

Importance to me: _____

_____

my perfectionism toolkit

Tools and techniques that help me when perfectionism is getting in my way:

Tool: _____ Page: _____

Description: _____

_____

Tool: _____ Page: _____

Description: _____

_____

Tool: _____ Page: _____

Description: _____

_____

Tool: _____ Page: _____

Description: _____

_____

Tool: _____ Page: _____

Description: _____

_____

Other insights, hints, or thoughts I want to remember:

_____

_____

_____

_____

_____

_____

a letter to my future self

Ann Marie Dobosz, MA, MFT, is a psychotherapist in private practice in San Francisco, CA, and mental health specialist for ReachOut USA. She has been passionate about youth health and well-being from her days as an editor at *Ms. Magazine*, where she focused on issues affecting teens and young adults. In her current work as a mental health professional, she specializes in helping people of all ages change unhealthy perfectionist patterns.

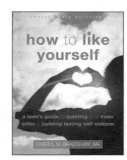

Register your **new harbinger** titles for additional benefits!

When you register your **new harbinger** title—purchased in any format, from any source—you get access to benefits like the following:

- Downloadable accessories like printable worksheets and extra content
- Instructional videos and audio files
- Information about updates, corrections, and new editions

Not every title has accessories, but we're adding new material all the time.

Access free accessories in 3 easy steps:

1. Sign in at NewHarbinger.com (or **register** to create an account).

2. Click on **register a book**. Search for your title and click the **register** button when it appears.

3. Click on the **book cover or title** to go to its details page. Click on **accessories** to view and access files.

That's all there is to it!

If you need help, visit:

NewHarbinger.com/accessories

new harbinger
CELEBRATING
40 YEARS